TAROT

BEGINNERS

A Guide to Psychic Tarot Reading, Real Tarot Card Meanings, and Simple Tarot Spreads

2nd Edition

LISA CHAMBERLAIN

Tarot for Beginners 2nd Edition

Copyright © 2019 by Lisa Chamberlain.

Published by **Chamberlain Publications**

ISBN-13: 978-1-912715-04-6

Disclaimer

No part of this publication may be reproduced or transmitted in any form or by any means, mechanical or electronic, including photocopying or recording, or by any information storage and retrieval system, or transmitted by email without permission in writing from the publisher.

While all attempts have been made to verify the information provided in this publication, neither the author nor the publisher assumes any responsibility for errors, omissions, or contrary interpretations of the subject matter herein.

This book is for entertainment purposes only. The views expressed are those of the author alone, and should not be taken as expert instruction or commands. The reader is responsible for his or her own actions.

Adherence to all applicable laws and regulations, including international, federal, state, and local governing professional licensing, business practices, advertising, and all other aspects of doing business in the US, Canada, or any other jurisdiction is the sole responsibility of the purchaser or reader.

Neither the author nor the publisher assumes any responsibility or liability whatsoever on the behalf of the purchaser or reader of these materials.

Any perceived slight of any individual or organization is purely unintentional.

YOUR FREE GIFT

Thank you for adding this book to your Wiccan library! To learn more, why not join Lisa's Wiccan community and get an exclusive, free spell book?

The book is a great starting point for anyone looking to try their hand at practicing magic. The ten beginner-friendly spells can help you to create a positive atmosphere within your home, protect yourself from negativity, and attract love, health, and prosperity.

Little Book of Spells is now available to read on your laptop, phone, tablet, Kindle or Nook device!

To download, simply visit the following link:

www.wiccaliving.com/bonus

GET A FREE AUDIOBOOK FROM LISA CHAMBERLAIN

Did you know that all of Lisa's books are available in audiobook format? Best of all, you can get **an audiobook of your choice completely free** as part of a 30-day trial with Audible.

If you'd like to learn divination, check out Lisa's *Tarot for Beginners*. The updated 2nd edition of this best-selling book covers the origins of Tarot, a comprehensive overview of the 78 cards and their meanings, and tips for beginning readers. Download for free here:

www.wiccaliving.com/free-tarot-audiobook

Or, if you'd like to learn another form of divination, try Lisa's best-selling *Runes for Beginners*, which covers the origins and meanings of these ancient mystical symbols, including their divinatory interpretations and their uses in magic. Simply visit:

www.wiccaliving.com/free-runes-audiobook

Audible members receive free audiobooks every month, as well as exclusive discounts. It's a great way to experiment and see if audiobook learning works for you.

If you're not satisfied, you can cancel anytime within the trial period. You won't be charged, and you can still keep your books!

CONTENTS

INTRODUCTION

The mysterious cards known collectively as the Tarot have experienced an explosion in popularity in the 21st century. Yet in the not-too-distant past, Tarot cards were mostly considered taboo in mainstream society, which is evident by their many appearances in horror movies. But any lingering fears about the Tarot are just a result of outdated ideas connecting anything remotely "pagan" or "occult" with nefarious or "evil" forces. Thankfully, as time goes on, society seems to become more and more enlightened about the nature of esotericism and alternative spiritual systems.

Tarot is also viewed by some religious people as a form of "fortune telling," which is forbidden in many sects of the world's major religions. Tarot certainly does have an association with the stereotypical image of the fortune tellers of old, one that emerged not long after the decks first came into use as playing cards for European nobles. But "fortune telling" is a very limited definition of what the Tarot is, and what it can provide for those who wish to discover its wisdom.

In fact, there's a crucial distinction to be made between fortune telling and *divination*. When you're having your fortune told, you're playing the role of the passive onlooker, helpless against the unpredictable twists and turns of life. You want to find out what *will* happen, as if the future were set in stone and there's nothing you can do about it. As a result, you're giving your power away to the forces of "fate," and believing that the fortune teller is the only one who can reveal that fate to you. This is not a very empowering place to be in. No wonder Tarot cards make some people nervous!

Divination, by contrast, is the art of accessing information, wisdom, and advice from the invisible realm—known variously as the ethereal plane, the astral realm, the unseen, or the *divine*. This is a realm we all have access to, as we ourselves are part of the interconnected Universe. The Tarot is a tool for understanding the language of this realm as it applies to our own life circumstances and development as spiritual beings. Viewed in this light, the Tarot experience can indeed be empowering, as it brings clarity to confusing situations and shows us that we have the ability to shape our future based on the choices we make in the present.

Many who work with the Tarot today describe it as a tool for meditation and reflection, for understanding the causes (and purposes) of the events that unfold in our lives, and for gaining insight and advice in decision-making. The cards can assist us as we navigate complex circumstances and plan our next moves, and show us new angles on situations that give way to broader perspectives. So, although you will learn about reading the cards for information about your future, this is not a book about fortune telling. There is much, much more to the Tarot than questions about what will happen next.

So what are these cards, exactly? Where did they come from, and how do they work? As is the case with just about any esoteric subject, none of these questions has a simple answer, and often the answers will depend on whom you ask. Nonetheless, if you're interested in learning about the Tarot, this guide will help you find your footing.

In Part One, you'll discover the history of this fascinating divination form, and a thorough introduction to the modern Tarot deck. Part Two offers tips and advice for learning to read the cards, and includes instructions for using two time-tested Tarot spreads. Part Three serves as a quick-reference guide to standard interpretations of each card in the deck.

By the end of this guide, you will be well on your way to practicing the art of Tarot reading. Keep in mind, however, that reading the cards is never as simple as reading a book. Your willingness to take your time learning the cards, to get plenty of practice, and to hone your intuition will be key to your development as a Tarot reader. But if you're willing to pursue this art in earnest, you will almost certainly find it to be a rewarding journey!

PART ONE

HISTORY
AND MYSTERY

THE SYMBOLIC LANGUAGE OF DIVINATION

Perhaps one of the most intriguing things about the Tarot is that it seems to be a product of both human invention and divine inspiration. Unlike other forms of divination that utilize simple tools like dice, or naturally-occurring phenomena like cloud watching, Tarot is a fairly complex affair involving many different interactive symbols originating in human culture.

Yet the Tarot has no single author or "original" deck. It is a divinatory art that was developed collaboratively over centuries, through the contributions of many people. There isn't even a comprehensive set of universally accepted interpretations for each card. Nonetheless, the Tarot offers limitless possibilities for finding clarity and meaning for those who seek the cards' assistance.

The Tarot can be thought of as a "language" through which we can hear and understand divine messages, whether we're reading the cards for ourselves or for others. Just as runes, tea leaves, or the lines of our palms each have a language that can communicate specific information, the Tarot—both the individual cards and the symbolic system of the deck as a whole—can show us much about ourselves and the world around us.

And this language is also still evolving, as each new generation of readers studies the theories and approaches of those who came before them and then adds their own perspective to the tradition.

This is part of the dynamic nature of this particular divinatory system.

Newcomers to Tarot often ask: Who, or what, is the guiding intelligence determining which cards you draw from the deck? Is there some kind of specific magical force inherent in the cards themselves? The truth is, no one can answer that question for you, because it depends on your individual beliefs and the unique way in which you understand and interpret the divination experience.

The cards can indeed behave in some seemingly magical ways, such as when a single card jumps out of the deck while you're shuffling, or when you pull a series of cards that are all astonishingly accurate to your situation. But—and this is important to know—you are also part of the equation. However you ultimately define the source from which the information comes, you yourself are connected to that source. You are tapping in to the wisdom of your own higher self, in conjunction with any other energies assisting in the reading.

If you're eager to get started tapping into that wisdom, you're free to skip ahead to the end of this guide and discover the basic meanings of each card in the Tarot deck. However, for a truly rich and informed understanding of how Tarot works, it's advisable to have some knowledge of where the Tarot comes from, as well as the basic functions of each type of card in the deck. You'll find all of this and more in the discussions below.

THE ORIGINS
OF THE TAROT

Some divination methods, such as scrying and watching the flight patterns of birds, are older than recorded history. Others, such as runes and palm reading, can be traced back at least to ancient times.

Tarot, by comparison, is a relatively new system of divination. It began to emerge in earnest in late 18th-century Europe, and was more substantially developed in the 19th and early 20th centuries. But the roots of Tarot—in terms of the structure and imagery of the deck as well as the esoteric wisdom contained within—go back much further.

Many myths, misconceptions, and scholarly debates about the history of Tarot abound today, and the full tale of its origins is beyond the scope of this guide. Instead, we'll take a brief tour of the main stages of its development, as this provides helpful context for understanding the Tarot today.

THE WESTERN MYSTERY TRADITION

During the 18th century, several French scholars and aristocrats began to take an interest in esoteric (or "occult") subjects like divination, magic, and alchemy. Like others in Europe had done over the course of many centuries, they were rediscovering and building on older philosophical and mystical traditions, including Jewish Kabbalah, Pythagorean theory and other Greek philosophy, and Hermetic teachings.

These and other elements of ancient and medieval spiritual exploration are collectively known as Western esotericism, or the "Western Mystery Tradition," which is still very much alive today. As we will see, various participants in this tradition have influenced our understanding of the Tarot as it has developed over time.

One such figure was Antoine Court de Gébelin, who in 1781 published an essay considered to be the first known work on the Tarot as a means of esoteric enlightenment. This inspired other "occultists," as such seekers were known, to expand on de Gébelin's ideas, and a few years later another Tarot enthusiast, Jean-Baptiste Alliete (who went by the name "Etteilla"), published the first guide to reading Tarot cards as a divination tool.

Several decades later, another highly influential occult scholar named Éliphas Lévi joined the efforts. Lévi's teachings on the Tarot, particularly in terms of its relationship to Kabbalah, are widely credited as being the most significant of his time, and his influence ultimately stretched into the 20th century and beyond.

MYTHS AND MISCONCEPTIONS

The French occultists contributed much to what we now consider to be "the Tarot," in terms of understanding its symbolism and its relationships with several different threads of esoteric knowledge. However, these seekers were also laboring under key assumptions about the Tarot that later proved to be historically incorrect.

First, they believed that the Tarot had originated in ancient Egypt. This was due partly to erroneous connections made between imagery on some of the cards and certain Egyptian artifacts, and partly to fabricated evidence being circulated among occult enthusiasts. It was also fashionable at that time to be able to connect everything having to do with esoteric knowledge back to ancient Egypt, so the notion that the Tarot was Egyptian was readily received.

A related belief was that the Tarot was brought to Europe by the people known to Europeans as "gypsies," who originated in India and began arriving in Europe during the Middle Ages. These nomadic people, more correctly identified as the Roma, were also mistakenly believed to hail from Egypt (hence the name "gypsies"), which obviously didn't help dispel the Egyptian origin theories. Later scholars, having more information about history and geography than these innovators of Tarot did, ultimately dismissed these ideas.

Today, many people argue that the Tarot had nothing to do with Egypt or gypsies, but was just an invention of the 18th-century occultists, who merely transcribed their existing esoteric knowledge onto what had been a mundane pack of playing cards. Yet this isn't an accurate assessment either. Actually, it turns out that while none of these origin theories is accurate, there is some truth to be found in each one.

For example, it is true that the Tarot deck as we know it today was modeled on playing cards used by the nobles of medieval society. These were somewhat like modern playing cards, in that they had four numbered suits, each of which had its own symbol.

The suits were typically known as batons, cups, swords, and coins. Each suit contained an Ace; a card for every number between two and ten, which are often called the "pip" cards; and four "face" cards, with a Knight in addition to the Jack (or Knave), Queen, and King. These cards were used to play various games known collectively as Tarot, which originated in Italy where they were known as *Tarocchi*.

At some point during the 15th century, a fifth "suit" was developed and added to these decks, which was entirely different from the others. This new suit consisted of several illustrated, un-numbered cards depicting scenes and figures which reflected Italian society, but which also appeared to be allegorical (or containing a hidden meaning).

These cards were known as *trionfi*, meaning "triumph," because they held more power in the game than the other cards. There were many different versions of the *trionfi*, and decks could vary widely in terms of the number and iconography of these cards. Eventually, the "triumph" cards became known as "trump" cards.

As noted above, it is commonly believed that these cards were used simply for entertainment purposes, and had no connection whatsoever to the esoteric ideas of the French occultists who would later attempt to link them to ancient Egypt. However, some scholars suggest that there was more to these Tarot decks than just card games for the wealthy.

There is evidence that as early as the 16th century, at least some of the cards from Tarot decks were being used for divination purposes, and even some church leaders in the mid-15th century used the imagery on some of the triumph cards to aid with philosophical and religious discussions.

Furthermore, the iconography on many of these "playing cards" was not without occult significance. During the time that the triumph cards were first being created, belief systems like Hermeticism, alchemy, and other esoteric philosophies were subjects of interest among the populace. But by the time the *trionfi* suit was added to the Tarot deck, the Roman Catholic Church had been cracking down on spiritual beliefs that contradicted its own doctrine.

To preserve what was quickly becoming "heretical" knowledge in the era of the Inquisitions, artists frequently created iconography that could still communicate esoteric ideas without overtly defying the Church's rules. Some believe that the imagery on the triumph cards was intended at least in part for this purpose, as they contained symbolism linked to the same sources—including ancient Egypt—that were inspiring what would come to be called the Western Mystery Tradition.

As for the gypsies, while they didn't invent the Tarot deck, they are not at all irrelevant to the story of the Tarot. The Roma brought their own belief systems and esoteric traditions with them, which, while distinctly different from that of Western esotericism, no doubt laid the groundwork for the emergence of Tarot as a divination form.

They were already readers of palms, tea leaves, crystal balls and clouds. They also had other divination forms that involved symbols, numerological associations, and a randomized process (like throwing dice or drawing lots) that they were able to adapt to a deck of cards. So as Tarot cards became more widespread in the 13th and 14th centuries, the "gypsies" incorporated them into their own divination traditions. Ultimately, the European occultists began to follow their lead.

MARSEILLE AND THE MAKING OF THE MODERN DECK

Until the invention of the printing press in the mid-15th century, playing cards would have been relatively difficult to come by, as decks were created by hand. This is why relatively few medieval Tarot cards have survived the centuries, and why there are so many differences among the earliest decks.

As printing technology became more widely available, the mass-production and standardizing of the Tarot deck got underway, particularly in the French city of Marseille. Here, the "triumph" cards were numbered with Roman numerals, in a relatively consistent order, and were given titles, such as "The Magician," "The Lovers," and "Strength."

By the end of the 16th century, this standardization was more or less complete, and though many different manufacturers created Tarot decks, all were very similar. This new "standard model" became known as the Tarot of Marseille (also spelled "Marseilles"), and the version of it most familiar to modern readers was first produced in 1748.

This was the deck that French occultists Antoine Court de Gébelin and Etteilla used as they explored the esoteric potential of the cards. As this period of discovery and innovation continued into the next century, the two different sections of the deck—the trionfi and the remaining four suits—came to be called "arcana," meaning "secrets" or "mysteries." This helped to popularize a concept of the Tarot as a divinatory art, distinct from its playing-card origins.

THE GOLDEN DAWN AND THE WAITE-SMITH DECK

Eventually, the Tarot came to interest British occultists of the 19th and early 20th centuries, in particular members of the Hermetic Order of the Golden Dawn, an organization founded in 1888 that came to heavily influence modern occultism in many ways. Here, occult scholars including Samuel Liddell MacGregor Mathers and William Westcott drew on the insights of Lévi and other earlier French occultists, but ultimately tweaked the deck to fit their own understanding of esoteric concepts and occult correspondences.

It was through this group that poet Arthur Edward Waite and artist Pamela Colman Smith came to create the most popular, and arguably the most influential, Tarot deck of the 20th century. It was based on the Tarot of Marseille, but with an important difference— it provided illustrations for the "pip" (numbered) cards. (One other known deck, from late-15th century Italy, had illustrated pip cards, and Smith drew some of her inspiration from visiting an exhibit of these cards while she was creating the new deck.)

This meant that rather than simply finding three cup symbols on the Three of Cups card, for example, one would instead discover three female figures with chalices in their hands, raising them together in what may be a ritual or a celebration. This imagery could open up more specific possibilities for interpretation than a simple pictographic image.

This was the first full Tarot deck designed exclusively for divination in the English-speaking world, and it's widely credited with popularizing the Tarot in the 20th century. It was initially known as the Rider-Waite deck, crediting the original publishers, William Rider & Son, but has more recently become known as the Waite-Smith deck, in order to give due credit to the artist responsible for the images on the cards.

THE EVOLUTION CONTINUES

Given all of the various phases of its development, from "everyday card game" to incredibly rich and diverse divinatory art, it's probably most accurate to say that the Tarot has no single "true" origin. Rather, it has always been a work in progress, a synthesis of wisdom, symbolism, and ideas with roots in many different cultures and time periods. And that work is by no means complete. Even though the Waite-Smith is still essentially the "standard" deck in the 21st century, many variations and even departures from it have arisen over the past several decades, as we will see later on.

As these newer decks have flourished, so have new systems and methods for interpreting the cards, which may or may not align with the interpretations popularized by the French and British occultists. Traditionally, occultists have argued for a specific set of interpretations that must be memorized in order to read the cards, but 21st-century mystics see these things differently, emphasizing intuition over rigorous study. Many also argue that as society develops and changes, so do the messages available in the Tarot, so sticking with the "old" meanings and methods can limit or skew our understanding of the cards.

These are important points to keep in mind, as the Tarot has been in a process of evolution since it first emerged. However, if you're new to the cards, it's helpful to get a good sense of the basic traditions before developing your own unique approach. So let's begin at the beginning, with an orientation to the Tarot deck as it has been known for the past century.

THE MODERN TAROT DECK

As we have seen, the standardization of Tarot decks that occurred in 18th-century Marseille ultimately gave rise to the structure of the Tarot as we know it today: a 78-card deck, comprised of 22 Major Arcana and 56 Minor Arcana cards.

The Minor Arcana is further divided into four suits, which retain the original structure of the four-suited card decks of medieval Italy: an Ace, nine pip cards numbered 2 through 10, and four Court cards.

The cards of the Major Arcana (or "greater secrets") generally reflect aspects of the inner self, the emotional and/or spiritual growth that we encounter along the journey of life, and significant events and turning points on one's individual path. By contrast, the cards in the Minor Arcana (or "lesser secrets") typically represent the more mundane elements of everyday life, through which we discover, experience, and apply the "lessons" represented by the Major Arcana.

The meanings associated with each card can be derived from one or more of many elements: the name of the card (especially within the Major Arcana), the number of the card (especially within the Minor Arcana), the card's illustration, and other details, as we will see shortly.

THE MAJOR ARCANA

The Major Arcana consists of 22 cards depicting a sequence of images: archetypal characters (The Emperor, The Hermit), celestial bodies (The Sun, The Star), objects (The Chariot, Wheel of Fortune), virtues (Judgement, Temperance), and situations (The Hanged Man, The Tower).

Traditionally, the cards are numbered in Roman numerals from I to XXI (1 to 21), with the remaining card, The Fool, either left unnumbered or given a "0." The ordering of the cards is consistent across decks, with the exception of the Justice and Strength cards (which will be explained below), and the position of the Fool, which is typically at the start of the sequence but can also be found at the end.

Various schools of interpretation for these cards have developed over time, with one approach often influencing another. However, the concept of the Major Arcana as representing a "journey" or "path" of some kind has been a recurring theme over the centuries.

In this framework, the cards may reflect the major events we encounter as we move through our physical lives, or they may represent our psychological or spiritual journey, as we experience the lessons our souls chose to learn during this present incarnation. In practice, the Major Arcana tends to address both physical and intangible aspects of our life experience.

Probably the most commonly used interpretive system for the Major Arcana today is what is called "the Fool's Journey." This term was made popular in the late 20th century by Tarot scholar Eden Gray, but the concept is likely inspired by the work of the Order of the Golden Dawn, as well as the writings of psychoanalyst Carl Jung and mythology scholar Joseph Campbell.

In this approach, the Fool is not a silly or stupid character. Instead, he represents the soul of each human being in its innate innocence, before it has embarked on the journey of life. The rest of the cards, laid out in order from 1 to 21, tell the story of what happens once the Fool steps forward into the journey of psychological or spiritual development.

The Fool will encounter both obstacles and victories, and meet many archetypal characters who will teach him important lessons along the way. The final card in the sequence is the World, signifying the fulfillment that comes with having learned and integrated the lessons he has encountered on his journey.

Of course, life's lessons rarely follow such a linear, storybook progression. Indeed, we can find ourselves in the position of the Fool in a number of different circumstances, such as starting a new job or new relationship, or encountering an intense emotional or psychological experience for the first time. This is why the Fool is not actually part of the overall sequence of the cards. Whether he's the first card or the last, he has no actual number and can fit in at any point in the sequence, as each card can be read in relation to him.

As for the rest of the cards, the order of the sequence is not meant to be proscriptive, since the stages of one's individual journey may take any order. Furthermore, the "journey" of the Major Arcana is cyclical, meaning that every time the Fool reaches the World, it's time to start again and learn something new. So the Fool's Journey concept can be thought of as a map, helping you identify where you are in the context of your situation, but it is not necessarily a set of directions.

There is no standard, universally-accepted set of interpretations for the Major Arcana in the context of the Fool's Journey, but many guides and seasoned Tarot experts offer sufficiently similar meanings to create a general consensus. As you familiarize yourself with the cards over time, you will no doubt come to your own understanding of each one, and how it relates to you on your own personal journey.

THE MINOR ARCANA

While the cards in the Minor Arcana may seem less significant than the "trump" cards, they actually represent the essential ingredients that make up our lives, without which, the lessons of the Major Arcana would have no context.

Each suit of the Minor Arcana is centered on a particular realm of experience: ideas, feelings, action, and manifestation. As these cards make up the bulk of the deck, they tend to be more prevalent in a reading than the Major Arcana cards.

In modern decks, the suits are most often known as wands, cups, swords, and pentacles, but some decks keep to the more traditional medieval names and symbols, while others have adapted different names and symbols altogether. The more widely used alternate suit names are listed beneath each suit description.

Wands

The suit of Wands represents the realm of inspiration, intention, and ambition. When we are feeling creative, inspired, spurred to action, and/or envisioning outcomes we are utilizing Wand energy.

There is a distinction to be made here between thought and action, however. Action is not yet dominant at the Wands stage, and sometimes this suit can remind us that enthusiastic beginnings still require follow-through. Wands also represent risk-taking and initiative, as we desire to grow, create, and expand our horizons. Because we are essentially motivated by desire—either to manifest a positive outcome or avoid a negative one—feelings of both apprehension and excited anticipation are connected to the cards of this suit.

On the whole, Wands are considered positive cards, and often show up in a reading as a sign of encouragement.

Also known as: arrows, batons, clubs, cudgels, rods, scepters, spears, staves

---

Cups

The suit of Cups is the realm of emotion, creativity, psychic insights, love, empathy, and matters of the heart in general. The Cups tend to represent the feelings that accompany, or arise out of, the thoughts we are having about a given situation. These feelings tend to influence our behavior, whether or not we're consciously aware of them.

A full range of emotions—both pleasant and unpleasant—is present within this suit, so some cards may appear to be negative, depending on the reading. Yet any cards that assist with getting clarity on a situation should be appreciated.

Cups can also speak to the benefits and potential pitfalls of psychic gifts and empathy. While an open and perceptive mind is generally an advantage, taking on other people's energy or getting overwhelmed by psychic impressions is not.

Also known as: bowls, cauldrons, chalices, goblets, hearts, vases, vessels

---

Swords

The suit of Swords represents the realm of action, movement, and struggle, as well as logic, reason, and intellect. The effort involved in pursuing a goal, which can often be perceived as struggle, is the realm of Sword energy. It can require much effort to turn our ideas into reality, but this is also where the most learning tends to occur.

Action is the result of the combining of ideas (Wands) with emotions (Cups), yet the Swords advise rationality and detachment from expectations of specific outcomes. Because of this, the cards of this suit can be perceived as cold or harsh with their messages, as they cut straight through any illusions we may be clinging to. In some cases, Swords may signify strength, authority, and power, as well as the more unfortunate elements of human nature that lead to violence and suffering.

The suit is not overwhelmingly unfavorable, but the Swords do tend to bring up the trickier aspects of a situation.

Also known as: arrows, athames, blades, daggers, feathers, knives, scimitars

Pentacles

The suit of Pentacles is all about manifestation, results, groundedness, and material well-being. These cards often appear in relation to issues of finances, abundance, business pursuits, and the home and family, as well as the physical body.

Pentacles represent the results of the initial inspiration (Wands), which is then responded to in the feeling realm (Cups), and consequently acted upon (Swords). While the other three suits predominantly inhabit the invisible realms of non-physical energy, Pentacles are concerned with the material, physical plane. However, they can also represent the feelings of security we all seek on the material plane, and the sense of being grounded in one's sovereignty as a person.

The cards of this suit are generally considered favorable, as they speak to the rewards of our efforts, but can also reflect fear around not having (or being) enough.

Also known as: circles, coins, discs, shields, stones, talismans

THE SIGNIFICANCE OF NUMBERS

As with many other forms of divination, numbers are highly significant in the Tarot. From the time of the modern deck's development in Marseilles, the number assigned to each card has been considered to be important to its meaning. In decks with non-illustrated pip cards, numerological correspondences are especially important to interpreting meaning. Each of these cards bears a number between 1 and 10—the number set at the core of numerology, also referred to as "the decad."

While different Tarot traditions may draw from one or more numerological systems (such as Pythagorean, Chaldean, or Kabbalistic numerology) when it comes to interpretation, the number descriptions below are representative of common themes and associations for each number in the decad. These core characteristics can help you get a clearer sense of how each numbered pip card is distinct from the others in its suit.

One is the beginning of that which is about to form or take shape. Represented by the Ace of each suit, it is considered to hold the "seed" or absolute potential of a situation. This potential may be dormant, and may even be unknown to you, just as a seed can be either intentionally planted or arrive unexpectedly on the wind. Either way, this potential needs further action and development for manifestation to take place, just as a single point in geometry needs another in order for a shape to take form.

Two is the necessary "next step" that allows the potential of the one to become something more. In geometry, where one point has nowhere to "go," two points make a line possible. In the Minor Arcana, these cards often depict two people, but this number can symbolize aspects of duality, polarity, balance, and choices as well as relationships.

Three represents the first fruition of the balanced union of the two. It is the synthesis of inspiration, cooperation and growth. Three points are the minimum required for the first closed shape— the triangle—to form. Three is also found three times (3, 6, 9) within the decad. It represents expression, creativity, manifestation, and integration. Three moves beyond partnership into group collaboration—beyond the balanced polarity of two into something more that requires a new, more complex balance—a pattern that will now begin to repeat through the rest of the numbers.

Four is a number of stability and completion. Added to the triangle of the three, it creates the first three-dimensional shape, the tetrahedron. In this sense the four is the manifestation of the initial idea of the one into material form. It represents balance, as seen in the four legs of a table, and secure foundations. Four is also associated with justice and fair dealings (as in the expression "fair and square"). Its metaphysical significance is seen in the four elements, the four cardinal directions, and the four seasons.

Five, like the three, is a number of outward expansion, coming along to disrupt the perfect symmetry of the four so that new manifestation can occur. The cycle of creation requires change, which is often disruptive and can cause uncertainty, difficulty and even chaos for periods of time. However, this imbalance spurs new movement, which opens up opportunities for new developments that could not arise otherwise.

Six brings order to the chaos of the five. Like the four, it is a number of balance and harmony, but since it integrates every stage of the one's manifestation thus far, its structure is more complex. As the first product of an odd and even number, it reconciles differences and restores equilibrium. Six represents successful adjustments to past challenges, and can often signify a victory. It represents the qualities of compassion and cooperation, responsibility, and service to others.

Seven is a number of strong mystical significance in spiritual traditions around the world. It is found in nature in the visible light spectrum, the planets visible from Earth, and the musical tones of the scale. We live in the rhythm of the seven through the days of the week. Seven creates a new dynamic out of the six by adding the one, creating new changes and opportunities. It represents choices, mystery, uncertainty, spirituality, wisdom, and the potential for perfection.

Eight brings back the energy of balance and symmetry, now as a double of the four. The continuous line of the eight resembles the symbol for infinity. There is stability on both the material and spiritual planes as circumstances harmonize with the cosmic order of the Universe. This brings new energy and power for accomplishing goals, organizing and integrating what has manifested so far, and bringing things nearer to completion. Eight represents progress, capability, regeneration, success, and personal power.

Nine is the final single digit, and as such symbolizes the end of a cycle, but in the numerological system of the decad, the final completion is still to come. Nine appears in every multiple of itself in the form of adding the digits in the multiple, representing the patterns of perfection found throughout the Universe. It is the triple of the three, a mystical and powerful configuration. It represents affirmation, culmination, and the surety of success, as well as boundaries, limits, and strength.

Ten contains the properties of the one, but now on a new level. As the final number of the decad, it completes whatever was left unfinished or unresolved in the nine, and sets the stage for the next cycle of manifestation to occur. Ten represents wholeness, fulfillment, and reaping the benefits of persistent effort. It is a number of resolution, consolidation, and readiness for new beginnings.

Having a sense of the esoteric meanings of individual numbers can add enormous depth to your understanding of the cards, especially when it comes to non-illustrated pips. But if you don't have experience with numerology, don't worry—you can still access interpretations for all of the cards, either through this guide, your personal deck's guidebook, or other sources on the Tarot.

If you find that a certain number or pair of numbers keeps showing up in your readings, however, it's worth looking up their esoteric meanings, as this signifies that the Universe is definitely trying to tell you something.

THE COURT CARDS

Also known collectively as the "Court Arcana," the four face cards of each suit (Page, Knight, Queen, and King) typically illuminate aspects of personality and character. They may represent actual people involved in a situation, but they often speak to the way people are *behaving* with respect to the situation, or to the personal qualities required in order to successfully navigate it.

Based on medieval European concepts of nobility, each court card has a rank within the hierarchy, with the Page at the "entry level" and the Queen and King at the top. These ranks signify various levels of experience and maturity within the domain that the suit represents—inspiration, emotion, action, or manifestation.

In this context, Pages represent younger people, who are just starting out in the realm of experience represented by the suit. For example, the Page of Pentacles may appear in a reading about a potential new job. Knights are more experienced in their respective realms, but are not always mature enough to know how to successfully channel their highly charged energy. The Knight of Swords, for example, may indicate that someone is acting rashly to achieve a goal without first considering all possible outcomes.

In regular playing cards, the King typically "outranks" the Queen, but in Tarot the two can be seen as the masculine and feminine embodiments of maturity and mastery over a situation. In this light, the Queen of Cups can represent the ideals of using emotional intelligence for the benefit of all, while the King of Wands may point to a wise and trustworthy counselor.

The Court Arcana can also refer to specific events or developments within the context of the reading. Pages, whose duties traditionally included running messages for the nobles they attended, often signify that news will be coming your way. Knights herald sudden action and/or a swift change in your circumstances. Queens represent creative ideas and plans becoming fully realized, while Kings signify a mastery of how you handle whatever comes your way.

As is the case with many other aspects of modern Tarot, not every deck uses the traditional names for the Court Arcana. Some decks substitute the Knave for the Page, while others use the Princess and Prince in place of the Page and Knight cards. This latter approach serves to balance out the gender representations, as opposed to the original face cards which contained three male roles with only one female role. Other modern decks may present Pages and even Knights as females in their illustrations as a means of creating balance.

ESOTERIC CORRESPONDENCES

So far, we have seen that each card in the Tarot deck has its own distinct symbolic meaning based on the archetype it speaks to (Major Arcana), the character or personality traits it represents (Court Arcana), or its suit and number (Minor Arcana). In addition to these core identifiers, other esoteric correspondences were integrated with the deck as it evolved in prior centuries.

As we saw earlier, Lévi perceived structural correlations between the Tarot and the esoteric traditions of Kabbalah (which by this point had been absorbed into the evolving Western Mystery Tradition as Hermetic Qabalah, apart from its Judaic religious context). He and other occult scholars viewed the 22 cards of the Major Arcana as being connected to the 22 letters of the Hebrew alphabet, which have their own esoteric meanings, and found correspondences in both the Major and Minor Arcana with the Kabbalistic Tree of Life spiritual tradition. Later, Waite and other Golden Dawn members attributed planets and zodiac signs to the Major Arcana cards.*

Many Tarot traditions still incorporate elements of Hermetic Qabalah to various degrees in their interpretations of the cards, and there are particular spreads and even decks that center on this connection. But the subject of Kabbalah/Qabalah is far too complex for the scope of this guide, and you don't need to understand it to read Tarot cards successfully.

Should you find yourself intrigued, however, it can be a rewarding option to explore further. In particular, those who study astrology may find that the planetary and zodiac associations can enhance your interpretations of the cards. For now, we'll just focus on the most significant and beginner-friendly realm of esoteric correspondences—the classical elements, which have also long been part of the metaphysical "fabric" of the Tarot deck.

The elements—Earth, Air, Water, and Fire—were seen by the ancient Greeks as the building blocks of everything within physical reality. Many other ancient cultures had similar concepts. While we now know this to be an oversimplification in the literal sense, we can still think of the elements as core energetic forces at play in our lives.

In the context of the Tarot, elemental associations can help shed further light on the situations we're asking about. Various occultists over time have assigned elements to both the Major and Minor Arcana, using different rationales and a variety of esoteric sources. As a result, these correspondences can differ from deck to deck, though there is a good deal of consistency as well.

The correspondences for the Major Arcana cards vary so widely that a discussion of them goes beyond the scope of this guide. However, the four suits of the Minor Arcana make for a natural fit with the four elements, and these correspondences, along with the numerological associations outlined earlier, can be particularly useful when it comes to the pip cards.

* In the process, they decided to reverse the order of the Strength and Justice cards. This move was not universally accepted, so today's decks may reflect either the original order of the Marseille deck or the revised order of the Waite-Smith deck.

The Suits and the Elements

In most traditions, Cups are associated with the element of **Water**, which always takes on the form of whatever contains it, and follows the path of least resistance. Water is also the realm of emotion. Cups cards, therefore, can speak to matters of the heart and/or psychic receptivity, and may advise us to open up to others or to establish useful boundaries.

Pentacles are associated with the element of **Earth**, as they relate to abundance, security, and the importance of being grounded in material reality. These cards often speak to issues related to money, career, and the home. However, they can also remind us to keep our feet on the ground in the midst of heightened mental and/or emotional activity, and to appreciate the physical experience of being alive.

Wands are most often associated with **Fire**, as the cards of this suit speak to the passion and energy that come with initiative and creative inspiration. Fire is the element of transformation, and Wands represent the "spark" of inspiration that is transformed into action and manifestation. However, some systems view inspiration as being in the realm of Air, which is also associated with thoughts, daydreaming, and other mental activity.

Swords are typically associated with **Air**, as they are seen metaphorically to cut through illusion and sharpen the intellect. They speak to using logic and reason to solve problems—all aspects of mental activity. Other traditions emphasize the *action* aspect of the Swords suit and therefore connect it to Fire, as it is ultimately action that transforms reality. The fact that swords are literally forged in fire also plays into this association.

MORE TO BE REVEALED

Now that you have a basic understanding of how the Tarot came into being, the structure of the deck, and how each type of cards can reveal different shades of meaning, it's time to take a hands-on approach to the cards.

In Part Two, you'll find tips for getting started with your own deck, an orientation to working with Tarot spreads, and some general advice on conducting successful readings. So read on if you're ready to start practicing the art of Tarot!

PART TWO

THE ART OF
READING TAROT

YOUR VERY OWN ORACLE

Traditionally, the act of divination was seen as the domain of a minority of people, those who had special abilities—the mystics, psychics, and mediums of the world. For millennia, communities had a designated role for a person with these gifts—the role of seer, soothsayer, or diviner.

People with questions about upcoming events, or about the underlying cause of some current misfortune, would go to the seer, who would perform the appropriate divination ritual and share the messages communicated from the spirit world. Although his tradition was largely driven underground in the West by the spread of Christianity, it never completely died out. So once the Tarot began to spread in influence, it was a natural choice for psychics and seers to adopt it into their practices. Today, reading Tarot is a thriving business for some who are highly adept at the art.

At the same time, more and more people are taking a "DIY" approach to the cards and learning how to read for themselves. This is somewhat of a break from tradition, which used to hold that if you wanted a reading, you were supposed to go to another Tarot reader, even if you were one yourself. This is perhaps part of the reason Tarot still has a slight aura of the "taboo" around it, as it suggests that the energy available in this form of divination could somehow be harmful.

While there are some considerations to be aware of before reading for yourself (which will be discussed later on), we each have our own ability to access divine wisdom, and the Tarot can be a highly effective tool for doing so. These days, rather than becoming professional readers, many people read for themselves exclusively, using the Tarot as a way of gaining personalized insight from the Universe as they navigate their daily lives.

The truth is, even if you aspire to learn to read Tarot for other people, it's rather impractical to expect to truly get to know the cards without practicing on yourself. And working with your own personal questions can help you establish a baseline understanding of each card, which you will ultimately build on as you experiment with different kinds of questions and different spreads. Over time, you will develop a highly individualized relationship with your cards, and this experience will aid you in any readings you do for others.

All this being said, going to an experienced reader—especially if you're brand-new to the Tarot—is an excellent idea. Getting a sense of how the overall process of a reading works, while not having to worry about how to interpret the cards, is a great first step for beginners.

But it's also good for more experienced readers to have someone else read for them, at least on occasion. An outside perspective can offer new angles of insight that you likely don't have access to when it comes to your own questions, no matter how objective you're able to be in self-readings. So if you can find a live, in-person Tarot reader, it's well worth treating yourself to a session.

If there are no readers in your area, try finding one who provides readings online. You can also look online for pre-recorded Tarot readings for your astrological sign. These are typically very generalized, as the cards are drawn for large groups of people rather than just you. But it can be a fun way to check out different reading styles, decks, and card interpretations as you grow in your own understanding of the Tarot.

The information in this section of the guide is presented from the assumption that you are primarily reading for yourself, though much of it also applies to reading for others. You'll find suggestions for choosing your own first Tarot deck, and strategies for getting familiar with each card. You'll then learn two standard spreads that serve as great starting points for your first few readings. You'll also find a step-by-step breakdown of the process of a reading, options for tailoring the approach to suit your unique style, and advice for getting the most out of reading the cards for yourself.

YOUR PERSONAL TAROT DECK

When it comes to the availability of Tarot decks, we are truly living in a Golden Age. Hundreds of different decks are commercially available, with new ones coming out all the time. Each deck has its own personality, mood, and style, and it's likely that no two decks will provide quite the same quality of reading experience.

The range of approaches among these decks—in terms of artwork, suit and card names, symbolism, and interpretations—surely goes beyond anything the French occultists of the 18th century ever imagined! Yet this unprecedented variety of decks can be overwhelming for those who are just starting out. When seeking your first deck, where should you even begin? Here are some points to consider as you browse your options.

FINDING THE RIGHT DECK FOR YOU

First, find out if there are any brick-and-mortar retail shops in your area that sell Tarot cards. If so, it's a great idea to go check them out in person. While most shops will not allow you to open the box and look through the cards, many do provide images of each card so that you can get a good sense of the overall aesthetic of the deck. Either way, you'll still get a feel for the size of the cards and the energy of the deck simply by holding the box in your hands, and you'll be able to compare at least a few decks against each other. You might also be able to ask the shopkeeper for recommendations based on your interests and experience level.

If you need to shop online for your deck, that's fine, too, and this may ultimately present you with more options. No matter which route you take, however, you'll want to view as many of the cards in the deck as possible before you commit. Often, you can find images of most, if not all, of the cards in more popular decks with a good internet search engine. It's very worthwhile to take this step. Otherwise, you run the risk of buying a deck based on the look of the card(s) featured on the box, only to open it and realize you don't care for the appearance of the majority of the rest of the deck.

In fact, the artwork on the cards is perhaps the most important aspect to consider when browsing Tarot decks. If you don't enjoy the visual aesthetic of the cards, you're not likely to have a positive experience with your readings. So make sure that the colors, imagery, and general feel of the cards resonates with you. Listen to your intuition as you examine each deck. If you don't feel drawn to the cards, then this is not the deck for you.

Another important factor, particularly for beginners to Tarot, is whether the images on the "pip" cards depict illustrations or just abstract designs. As we saw earlier, Illustrated pips, such as those found in the Waite-Smith deck, can allow for a wider range of interpretation than pips that simply depict the number of the suit (such as 3 swords, 4 cups, or 5 wands), with no accompanying scene or story. For those who are less visually oriented and/or those who resonate strongly with the symbolic meanings of numbers, non-illustrated pips can work just fine. This is a personal choice, but definitely one to put some thought into before committing to a deck.

Finally, most beginners benefit from choosing a deck that comes with an instruction booklet. Since each deck is unique, the shades of meaning for each card can differ from those presented in the Waite-Smith or other more traditional decks. A booklet can help you get acquainted with the creator's vision for these specific versions of the cards. It's true that most booklets contain very brief card meanings, but some deck creators have begun to go above and beyond the norm by including detailed guides that are closer to full-fledged books in length and size. Booklets of any length also tend to include a model spread or two.

If your deck does come with a booklet, you may find that there are both similarities and differences when compared to the card meanings provided in this guide. Similarities can strengthen your overall concept of each card, while conflicting interpretations offer an opportunity to further develop your intuition. The conventional wisdom is to always go with the interpretation that comes from your deck's instruction booklet, but if yours only provides two or three words per card, this may not prove very helpful. In these situations, look to the cards surrounding the card in question for more guidance, and as always, listen to your intuition.

DEPARTURES FROM TRADITION

The explosion of interest in Tarot has led to many fascinating innovations on the "traditional" Marseille and Waite-Smith decks. Some use different names for the suits, such as "disks" for pentacles, "athames" for swords, etc.

Many deck creators have reimagined the Major Arcana as well, keeping the number and order of cards the same but naming the figures differently. For example, the card known as "The Devil" in the traditional decks might be called "Materialism," "Ego," or even "Nature," depending on how the creator of the deck views the role of that particular card. In decks that reflect a specific cultural and/or spiritual orientation, such as Norse or Native American, the figures in the Major Arcana may even be adapted to represent specific deities.

Some publishers have created "novelty" decks that revolve around specific themes, occult traditions, and even aspects of popular culture, like television shows. These decks range from the delightfully eclectic to the downright silly, and some in the latter group may be more suitable as collector's items than as tools for actual readings.

Broadly speaking, however, each departure from the more standard decks provides an opportunity to expand into new realms of meaning within the overall world of the Tarot. Still, if you're just starting out, it may make more sense to stick with something in the more traditional category, and branch out to more unusual decks once you get more experience.

What if you find you just can't settle on one Tarot deck? What if two or more seem to be calling to you? By all means, get as many decks as you'd like. Many readers of Tarot keep several different decks, which they might choose from according to their mood or for a particular type of reading.

However, when you're just beginning, it's typically best to use the same deck as you work your way through the process of learning the cards and getting familiar with a few spreads. So choose just one to begin with, and when you begin to feel reasonably confident at reading, then feel free to branch out to other decks.

GETTING ACQUAINTED WITH YOUR CARDS

The Tarot is like a complex and endlessly interesting new friend. It will take awhile to get to know your cards, and there will be more and more information revealed as you deepen your relationship. So take your time, and enjoy the unfolding!

For your first "meeting," try fanning the cards out in front of you, or briefly flipping through the deck so you get at least a glimpse of each card. Typically, brand-new decks come with all the cards in order, starting with the Major Arcana and then proceeding through each suit of the Minor Arcana. You may want to spread out one suit at a time, beginning with whichever one sparks your curiosity the most. Take a look at the progression of the suit, beginning with the Ace and moving through to the King. Do the same with the Major Arcana, starting with the Fool and moving through to the World.

Then, spend some time taking in each card in the deck individually, without focusing on the suit it belongs to. Study the imagery, making an effort to notice the small details. Then move slowly through another round, this time familiarizing yourself with each card's given meanings as you study it. Of course, with 78 cards, this is too big a task to be accomplished all in one sitting. Try setting some time aside once a day, and work your way through 5 to 10 cards at a time.

You can also connect with your deck on an energetic level, rather than a cerebral level. Some people actually place their cards underneath their pillow at night, to aid the subconscious in absorbing the meanings of the cards while they sleep. You could try this with the whole deck, or else "sleep on" one card at a time. This can be especially useful for those cards that just seem harder to get a clear sense of no matter how much you study them.

Another way to enhance your connection with your new cards is to clear them of any impersonal or unwanted energy, and then charge them with your own energy. Clearing is highly recommended, as the deck will have been handled by various people along its journey from the manufacturer to your hands. This energetic residue is not necessarily negative, but it's a bit like "dust" that can partially obscure your inner eye's view of the cards.

To clear your cards, you can pass the deck through the smoke of sage or other purifying herbs, lay it out under the light of a full moon, or ring a bell or chimes near it to clear out old vibrations. (For best results, remove the cards from the box and/or any other packaging first.) To charge your cards, hold them in your hands and visualize your energy moving through your fingers and into each card in the deck. You may want to see the energy as a blue, indigo, violet, or white light. Alternatively, you can lay the cards in moonlight, which acts as both a clearing and charging agent, or set the deck on a quartz crystal or pentacle slab and visualize each card vibrating with clear, clean, positive energy.

Take care to be deliberate about how and where you store your cards when you're not using them. Like anything else, the cards will absorb energy no matter where they are, and if they are neglected or treated carelessly, the quality of your readings will likely begin to reflect this.

Some people believe that their cards will have more divinatory clarity and power if they are kept inside of a special pouch or box. Others like to keep them stored with a specific type of crystal, such as clear quartz or blue sodalite. This all comes down to personal preference, of course—the main thing is that you maintain respectful care of the cards both when using them and storing them.

A METHOD FOR DISCOVERING MEANINGS

The following is a helpful practice for opening up to the potential messages of your new cards, by studying each card in detail. Because it relies exclusively on visual clues, it isn't ideal for non-illustrated pip cards. If the Minor Arcana in your deck doesn't contain illustrations of people or scenes, you might want to pull all the Major Arcana cards out and work with them separately.

1. Begin by identifying a question—something you can't know the answer to for certain, but want to know. This could be about a relationship, a career decision, or simply a "forecast" request for the day or week ahead. Keep in mind that you'll only be working with one card, which is rarely enough to provide insight on complex questions, so try to keep it simple. (You'll

find more details about forming useful questions later on.) Also, avoid questions you feel strong emotion about, as this can distract you from the primary purpose of the exercise, which is noticing details and allowing your receptive mind to open up. Write your question down on a slip of paper, fold it up, and set it aside. Shuffle your deck for a moment, cards facing away from you, staying focused on your question. When you feel ready, select a card at random. Set the rest of the deck aside, and let go of the question.

2. Turn the card over to reveal it, then quickly turn it back. Now, what is the main thing you remember? What stood out as your very first impression? For example, if you drew the 3 of Wands from the Waite-Smith deck, you might first notice the back of the figure in the center of the card, and possibly a vague sense that there are three long staffs surrounding the figure. Close your eyes and make a mental note of whichever detail(s) you can still see without looking at the card.

3. Now turn the card back over again and take a moment to look at the whole picture. What else do you see? Using our example card, you might this time identify the figure as a man, and take in his right arm holding one of the staffs. What do you *feel* as you continue to look at the card? Does the imagery seem to depict a peaceful feeling? A sorrowful one? Pay attention to any "gut feelings" that arise, no matter how subtle. This is your intuition, activated by the energy of the card.

4. Next, spend a couple moments zooming in on the smaller details. With the 3 of Wands, you'll see that the figure is facing what looks to be a desert, with a mountain range in the background. A green swath of fabric hangs over the figure's left shoulder. What other colors are present? What other details do you see, however minute?

5. After you've spent time with each detail, "zoom out" and take another look at the picture as a whole. Imagine the image as a frozen scene in a larger story. Try to discern what the action is.

What is happening? *Why* might it be happening? Is this man about to cross this wide open land? Or has he possibly just come from crossing it, and is now looking back on how far he's come? Use the details as clues. What messages might this card be trying to communicate, based solely on what you see? If you can, describe what you're seeing out loud, and/or jot down your impressions in a notebook.

6. When you've given the card a thorough consideration, taking note of every detail and every intuitive "hit" that may have come through, unfold the question you asked at the beginning of this exercise. Think about your observations of the card in light of this question. Which of the details and/or possible messages seem significant? Which do not? Feel free to explore this for as long as you would like. Pay attention to the difference between how it feels to try to "figure out" an interpretation with your thinking mind, and how it feels to simply receive impressions that flow effortlessly into your awareness.

If, after quite some time, you don't experience any kind of "hits," try again with a new card. You might try drawing different cards until you land on one that really pulls your interest, and/or try a different question. Consider using this approach with one card per day until you've worked your way through the deck.

REVERSED CARDS

Many Tarot traditions work with the concept of "reversed" cards, which are cards that appear upside down (from the querent's perspective) in a reading. Reversed cards can be interpreted to have the opposite meaning from their upright position, but in practice it's not always quite that simple. For example, when a card's upright meaning is negative or unfavorable, the reversed meaning may simply be a more intense degree of the same interpretation. Alternatively, a reversed card may emphasize a specific angle of the theme represented by the card as a whole.

Readers who use reversed cards find that they can add an extra depth to the reading that can't be discovered if all the cards are facing the same way. However, there are plenty of readers who don't use reversed cards, choosing instead to emphasize the position of the card in the spread, the card's overall theme, and its interplay with the other cards to determine which aspect(s) of the card's potential meaning to zero in on. This approach can help avoid interpreting one's situation in an unnecessarily negative manner, while still highlighting any potential problems, issues, or needed changes that the cards are pointing to.

Whether to use reversed cards in your readings is entirely up to you. When you're just starting out, there's plenty to learn just from using the upright meanings, so you might consider waiting until you're more experienced before deliberately incorporating reversed meanings. That being said, studying reversed meanings can help you get a more clearly defined sense of each card's overall energy, purpose, and message.

And there's no need to shy away from reversed cards simply out of fear of "bad news." For one thing, reversed meanings often simply indicate a "lack of good news," or a delay in events you're anticipating. But more importantly, Tarot is about *reflection* rather than *prediction*, assisting you with understanding and then navigating situations in order to bring about the best possible outcome.

WORKING WITH TAROT SPREADS

A spread is an established pattern for laying down the cards, with each card placed in a specific location and in a specific order. Each position in the pattern provides a particular angle on the situation that the *querent* (the person seeking the reading, whether this is you or someone you're reading for) is asking about. Spreads provide a means of conversing with the cards and help us to "organize" their messages into a useful framework for understanding various aspects of the question at hand.

Some Tarot readers argue that the more complicated the spread, the more difficult the required skill level will be, but this isn't necessarily true. In fact, the Celtic Cross spread, which we will detail below, is often recommended for beginners, as it provides a good example of how the cards in different positions relate to each other to provide a more comprehensive reading. But first, we'll look at the classic three-card spread, which is an excellent one to work with for your first few readings.

THE THREE-CARD SPREAD

The Three-Card spread is perfect for finding answers to relatively simple questions, and makes for a good practice layout when getting acquainted with a new deck. It can be done fairly quickly, so you can seek answers "on the fly" when needed. The number three has always had special significance in occult symbolism, as well as in many other religious and mystical traditions.

Traditionally, the Three-Card spread provides an "at a glance" view of the querent's past, present, and future with regard to a specific context. In this layout, the present is the card in the center, the past is the card on the left, and the future is on the right. The cards laid down either from left to right, or, in some traditions, beginning in the center, then left, then right.

Whether to begin in the center or on the left is a personal preference. Reading the present card first can reveal the angle of the situation the cards are speaking to, which might help you see the past in a new light. Conversely, starting with the past can help you confirm that the cards are answering the question you asked in a way that makes sense to you. Go with your instincts here, or try both approaches to see which works best for you.

Beyond this timeline-oriented reading, the three-card spread can also be tailored to fit a variety of approaches to the querent's question. Each card can represent a particular aspect of the topic at hand, and you can designate the meanings of the positions to answer specific questions about it.

For example, if you're trying to decide whether or not to take a specific action, you can have the card on the left represent what happens if you do and the card on the right represent what happens if you don't. The card in the middle can represent advice on making your decision.

Here are a few more examples of possible three-card spreads:

Morning (or evening) daily reading

1. The dominant energies of the upcoming day
2. Advice for navigating those energies
3. The outcome if advice is followed

Understanding a relationship

1. You in the present moment
2. The other person in the present moment
3. The connection between you

A self check-in

1. Your physical body
2. Your emotional state
3. Your spiritual/energetic landscape

However you design your three-card spread, just be sure to be clear about what stands for what in your own mind as you choose and lay down the cards. It can be helpful to identify the position as you lay the card down, so that, for example, as you lay down card #1 you say "The energies of the day" aloud.

This spread can be also used in a general reading with no specific question, but it may not be ideal for this purpose since there isn't much scope for detailed information—in other words, without a question, it may be difficult to determine what aspect of the querent's life the cards are pointing to.

THE CELTIC CROSS SPREAD

The Celtic Cross incorporates aspects of the Three-Card spread, but goes well beyond the past, present, and future positions to provide a much more detailed and nuanced picture. The cards are laid out to resemble a square cross (hence the name), accompanied by a four-card vertical line to the right.

First brought to the occult community through the Golden Dawn, the Celtic Cross has evolved over time into many different versions. (In fact, if you look online for examples, you may not even find two that are exactly alike.) Most use ten cards, but a few use eleven, and the order and titles of the positions can vary widely.

The version below represents a fairly standard ten-card spread, with commonly used position designations. Try using this version for a reading or two, and then experiment with other variations until you find one that works.

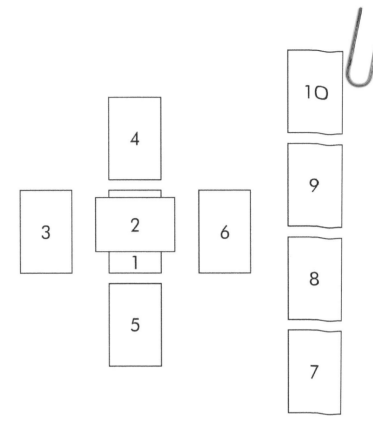

1. **Self.** Reflects the querent's state of mind regarding the question and/or how they are viewing themselves with regard to the situation.

2. **Situation.** Reflects the primary concern of the reading for the querent. It sits on top of and "crosses" the Self card, because it typically represents a quandary the self feels hindered by. This may involve making a decision, being confused about something, or wanting to change something. Whatever the situation, the rest of the cards in the reading will add up to bring about an expanded view of it.

3. **Recent Past.** Represents the past and events that are departing from the present focus. This card can shed light on what happened that brought about the situation. It also serves to

confirm for the querent that the cards are speaking to their question, as it usually reflects an identifiable event or feeling that the querent has recently experienced.

4. **Higher Guidance.** Represents the querent's higher self and the guidance that is available when the querent takes a bird's eye view of the situation. Can indicate the life lessons or opportunities for development of the soul that are arising through the situation.

5. **Foundational Influences.** Indicates influences that form the root of the querent's experience of the situation. These can include unexamined beliefs, memories, lessons learned from prior experiences, and possibly repressed emotions, as well as the wisdom and useful knowledge the querent has acquired thus far on their life journey. This card often reveals information that the querent isn't consciously aware of and may require a willingness to look at one's "shadow side," but the insight gleaned will be worth it.

6. **Near Future.** Represents events that will soon be taking place. This is not indicative of the overall outcome, but rather the next step in the unfolding situation. It can be seen as an advantageous heads-up, and, if unfavorable, a possible opportunity to quickly change course based on the information and advice from the rest of the cards.

7. **Hopes and Fears.** Represents the querent's hopes, dreams, and fears about the future with regard to the situation. Hope and fear are often two sides of the same coin, as one represents the wanted outcome and the other represents the unwanted. This card can often help reveal the hidden fears that are holding the querent back from achieving a goal, such as the paradoxical fear of getting what one desires.

8. **External Influences.** Reflects the atmosphere and influences— the people, events, and energies—immediately affecting the querent and/or the situation. This card often points to outside

factors that are out of the querent's control. It may also reflect the perspective(s) of others involved.

9. **Advice.** Indicates what the querent should do (or stop doing) in order to bring about a desired outcome, or at least avoid or minimize an unwanted outcome. This card may advise specific action, but can also illuminate a useful perspective to adopt or a message to keep in mind as the querent navigates the situation.

10. **Potential Outcome.** Indicates the long-term outcome of the situation based on the other cards in the reading, and is often interpreted by the querent as the answer to the question that prompted the reading. However, this card is only an indication of what is likely to happen based on the querent's current approach to the situation. The future is never set in stone, so if the Outcome card is not favorable, it is always in the querent's power to change course. Review the reading as a whole and zero in on the cards that signify what the querent can do to manifest a better outcome. It may also help to draw another card or two if clarification or additional information is needed.

There are many different kinds of established spreads to choose from beyond these two classics, so be sure to research further options on your own. Spreads can range from a simple one-card reading to layouts that involve 12 or more cards. Depending on the question at the heart of the reading, some spreads are likely to be more useful than others. So don't be afraid to experiment with different possibilities until you find one that works for you.

ANATOMY OF A TRADITIONAL TAROT READING

Although you may be mostly (or entirely) reading Tarot for yourself, it's still useful to learn about how a traditional reading (between a reader and a querent) unfolds. Then you can tailor your own approach as you see fit. There are actually many variations of each step along the way, as this is a highly individualized intuitive art, but what follows is a basic outline of the process.

PREPARING FOR A READING

First, the environment in which a reading takes place is an important consideration. It probably goes without saying that there should be no outside distractions to interrupt the flow of information coming through to both the reader and the querent. But creating an ambience that facilitates a clear and insightful reading is also advisable.

Smudging the space with sage or other purifying herbs can do wonders to clear the air of "psychic static," or any unwanted energies that might otherwise be attracted to the opening of one's sixth-sense receptivity. This isn't necessary for every single reading, especially in a space that is consistently used for readings, but it can be a helpful enhancement.

A designated surface for laying out the cards is ideal. This can be a special cloth or small tapestry used directly on the floor, or a cleared-off table with no extraneous objects (phones, piles of mail, etc.) to clutter up the energy of the reading. Candles and a crystal or two are also a nice touch, but are not strictly necessary. The main thing is to establish a space that is conducive to focusing on the cards and the messages they offer.

Equally important is for the reader to be grounded and centered before the reading begins. This might involve smudging the reader's body and the area just above their head, spending a few moments in quiet mediation, visualizing a protective circle of white light around the reading space, speaking words of intention for a successful reading, or a combination of any of these methods. This step helps ensure that the reader can stay focused amid the often "swirling" effect of the psychic impressions that come through as the cards are revealed and considered.

FRAMING THE QUESTION

Typically, people seek a Tarot reading because they want to know about some specific issue or aspect of their lives, whether it's in the outer realms of work, money, family, etc. or the inner realms of emotional and psychological well-being, self-discovery, and spiritual development.

This isn't always the case, however, and it's perfectly fine to just pull cards for a "general" reading and see what comes up. But for those just starting out, having a question to serve as the focal point of the reading helps to narrow down the possible interpretations of any given card, and gives a distinct shape to the messages coming through.

Another benefit is that framing a question causes you to get more clear on what it is you want to know before the reading begins. And there is definitely an art to phrasing the question in an advantageous way. For beginners, it's generally best to avoid "yes or no" questions, as it can be difficult to interpret the cards in a clear-cut manner in this type of reading.

There aren't any cards in the deck that mean "yes" or "no" in a literal sense. So, for example, "Will I get a new job this year?" is not an ideal question. Instead, you might try "What is there to know about my career situation in the near future?" or "How might I best go about finding a new job?" Basically, you're looking for a blend of specificity and open-endedness that allows the cards to enlighten you through their unique language of symbolism and suggestion.

The first word of your question can help you see whether you're on the right track. For example, "Who" and "When" questions are often tough (though not impossible) to get clear answers to. By comparison, "How" "What" and "Why" questions can open things up for tremendous insight.

The querent may or may not communicate the question to the reader, depending on the preferences of either person. Some readers find it helpful to know what the focus of the reading will be in the querent's mind, while others prefer to interpret the cards "blindly," to ensure they're not letting their own sense of logic interfere with the intuitive process.

Some querents may feel their question is too personal to share with the reader, preferring to keep their thought process private over the course of the reading. Others like to let the focus of the reading be out in the open and will often volunteer more information as the cards bring different aspects of the situation to light. In this situation, provided there is sufficient trust on the querent's part, the conversation that unfolds between the reader, the cards, and the querent can greatly enhance the clarity of the reading.

SHUFFLING, CUTTING, AND DRAWING THE CARDS

Next to the actual interpretation of the cards, shuffling the deck is perhaps the most important step in the overall reading process, as this is the act that signals to the Universe that communication is being sought.

Shuffling should always occur before a reading, even if you're just quickly pulling a card for yourself on a whim. Otherwise, energetically speaking, you're really just looking at "yesterday's news." Shuffling is important for physically reordering the cards in a randomized way, but also for the *metaphysical* act of intending for a successful reading while physically handling the cards.

There are several ways to approach shuffling the cards, and differing theories on who, in a traditional reading, should be doing the shuffling. Some readers prefer that no one else's personal energy come into physical contact with their cards, and will therefore always shuffle the deck themselves. Others want the querent's energy to mix with that of the deck so that the cards will be more responsive to the individual's specific circumstances. Still others work with a blend of the two approaches, having the querent shuffle the cards for a moment, and then taking the deck back to finish the job themselves.

If there is no stated question for the reading, then the person shuffling the cards can simply intend for a clear and useful reading in general terms. If the querent is shuffling and has an unstated question, they can focus on their question, repeating it silently over and over as they handle the cards. If the question is stated, then either person can focus on it while shuffling, but the reader may still prefer to keep a general intention for a successful reading. The cards are shuffled until the person shuffling feels that the time is right to stop.

As for how to shuffle the cards, there are plenty of methods, from flashy casino-style shuffling to spreading the cards face down on the table and picking them back up randomly, one at a time. There's no right or wrong way to do this. Just make sure that the cards are getting sufficiently moved around so that at least most of them have shifted places in the pile, and trust the process. If you're including reversed cards in the reading, you can shuffle in a manner that ensures that some cards will end up upside-down in the deck.

After shuffling, it's traditional to "cut" the deck, though not all readers do this for every type of reading. The deck may be cut once, twice, or three times, depending on personal preference. The cards are typically split into piles (face-down) and then put back together in a new order before they are drawn.

How the cards are drawn also varies widely. Many readers draw all the cards and place them in position in the spread themselves. Others have the querent draw and show them where to place each card to create the spread. The entire deck may be fanned out to draw from randomly, or the stack may be kept intact to draw from off the top, one card at a time, until all the cards required for the spread have been drawn. In some readings, the deck may be in two or three piles, each of which is drawn from in turn. You'll want to experiment with various methods to see what works best for you.

TURNING AND READING THE CARDS

As for when to turn the cards over to reveal their images, this also varies among readers. Some like to flip each card as it's drawn and then lay it face-up in its position in the spread. Others keep the cards face-down until the whole spread is laid out.

At this point, they might turn all the cards at once, to get a general overview of the spread before they start reading each card individually. This can be particularly helpful for getting a sense of how the cards are interacting with each other, before diving into the specifics.

But others prefer to turn over and contemplate one card at a time, like reading and absorbing one chapter of a story at a time before moving onto the next. Again, experimenting with all of these options can help you determine what works best for you.

No matter which approach you take, however, be sure to spend time lingering over the full spread after each card has been considered. This is a good opportunity to look for patterns, such as repeating numbers, many cards from a particular suit, and how different cards may relate to each other in terms of imagery or themes.

If there are several Major Arcana cards, for example, then it's likely that you are (or soon will be) dealing with particularly important events or energies. If you have a predominance of certain numbers or suits, take a look back at the general descriptions for those in Part One of this guide for additional insight.

CLOSING THE READING

When it seems that the cards have had their say in this particular reading, and the querent has sufficient new insight or information to reflect on, the reading can be brought to a close. (In the case of professional Tarot readings, this might also be determined by the time on the clock, though readers do try not to stop abruptly in the middle of an important discussion.)

The querent may make some notes, either mentally or in a journal, to contemplate over the next few days or weeks. (Taking a picture of the reading to refer to later on can also be useful.) The cards are then inserted randomly back into the deck, and the deck is typically shuffled to "reset" its energy for the next reading.

READING FOR YOURSELF

As mentioned earlier, reading the cards for oneself was once thought to be an unwise undertaking. And while it seems that the overwhelming majority of Tarot readers—both new and experienced—have dispensed with this notion in recent decades, there are still some elements to consider when you read your own cards.

Perhaps the main difference between reading for yourself and reading for others is the level of objectivity and detachment you're able to maintain. When it's someone else's reading, it's fairly easy not to be personally concerned with which cards turn up and what they have to say. But our own readings can be another story altogether. You may be unconsciously inclined to interpret your cards in a favorable light, stretching or even changing the meaning you normally associate with a given card until it fits with what you want the "answer" to be.

Be watchful for this tendency—it's only human nature to be attached to certain outcomes, but it isn't doing you much good to ignore what the cards are trying to tell you. In fact, you may end up limiting the depth of your general understanding of the cards and all of their possible interpretations if you're trying to "make" them mean what you want them to mean.

Of course, your degree of objectivity and intuitive receptivity will depend on your question. If you're seeking guidance on a fairly mundane decision, especially when both choices are acceptable to you, then you're likely to be receptive to clear messages. But if the matter is near and dear to your heart, or if you're really hoping for a particular answer, it can be difficult not to try to read the cards in a way that conforms to your desired outcome.

If you find yourself looking simply for confirmation of what you hope to hear, or if you find yourself scrapping the reading and starting over in hopes for "better" cards (and surely most of us have been quite tempted to do so!), this is definitely a sign that you're not detached enough from your question to get a clear reading at this time. So as you're starting out, it's a good idea to work with questions you don't have a lot of personal attachment to.

Another challenge for beginners is, of course, self-doubt. Because there are so many cards to learn, it can be easy to come up empty when it comes to interpreting any given card, or even an entire reading. But doubting your ability to accurately interpret the cards can and will get in the way of your openness to messages from the invisible realms. Let it be okay with you if one or more cards aren't crystal clear at first. You do need to practice and allow for a certain amount of trial and error.

This is why it's a good idea to consult the given meanings in your deck's booklet, and/or other Tarot guides like this one, at least until you feel you've achieved a certain amount of fluency with your deck. Don't worry about being over-reliant on guidebooks at the outset. That being said, do leave room for your sixth sense to do its work.

Experimenting with self-reading provides you an opportunity to recognize and allow intuitive "hits" rather than pushing for a logical interpretation. If a certain message or interpretation suddenly "appears" in your mind as you study a card, take note of it, and observe how this experience feels in comparison to looking up the meaning in your guide.

Finally, in a self-reading, there's the potential for fear around any information that is perceived as unwanted or negative, particularly as it relates to questions about the future. In fact, while the usual tendency is to put a favorable spin on the cards, some beginners may actually be prone to do the opposite, and wind up expecting all kinds of misfortune as a result.

Once again, this is where objectivity is key, so if you find yourself getting worked up over the cards in your spread, take a break and come back to the subject later when you've had some distance from it. And if you haven't already, be sure to ground and center yourself (as discussed earlier) as well, so you're not dealing with unwanted or distracting energies.

This is also where the concept of reflection rather than prediction comes becomes especially important. The cards only ever reflect probabilities based on where you are at any given moment in time. And unlike the weather forecast, if you don't like what lies ahead, you can ask the cards for advice on how to change course.

Ultimately, never forget that we create our reality—with our visions for our future, with our habits of thought about the present, and with our actions. We often can't control our circumstances, but we can control how we respond to them, and therefore ultimately utilize them to our advantage. Tarot is a tool for gaining wisdom and advice for how to do just that.

MEANINGS AND MASTERY

The art of Tarot takes time and experience to master. Over time and with practice, the meanings of the cards will come to you more easily—beginning with those cards you tend to draw with a lot of regularity, and ultimately including the rest of the deck as well. Until then, you can always rely on established card meanings to help you, whether through a booklet accompanying your deck, or a guide like this one.

In Part Three, you'll find general but illuminative descriptions of each card's meaning. Don't feel the need to try to memorize them right now. Simply pick a few cards to learn about first, and then follow where your intuition leads you!

PART THREE

MEANING
OF THE CARDS

THE SUBTLETIES
OF INTERPRETATION

Here you'll find keywords and brief descriptions for each card in the standard Tarot deck, for both upright and reversed positions. While these meanings are accurate in a general sense, it's important to realize that each deck has its own unique approach to the Tarot that may lead to differences from the interpretations you find here.

For example, the imagery on each card is important to pay attention to, as it will offer you more nuanced meanings and messages than the title of the card alone can provide. (Since there is such a wide variety of imagery in Tarot decks these days, often departing completely from the images found in the Waite-Smith deck, this guide presents general meanings based only on each card's title.)

The position of the card in the spread of the reading is also significant to the card's interpretation. (For a very basic example, the meaning for a card in the "past" position should not be read as if it were still true in the present, even though it may be written that way in the guide.)

Furthermore, other cards in the spread may alter or shift the general meaning provided here. As you gain more experience, you'll begin to see the subtleties within each reading that help you which angle of the card is currently applicable. For now, the information below provides a baseline from which to get more familiar with the cards of the Tarot.

THE CARDS OF THE
MAJOR ARCANA

0
THE FOOL

Origins, journey, a leap of faith, innocence, new beginnings, wonder, imagination. A new adventure is about to be underway, with plenty of unknowns along the path. This card represents the primal and unpredictable energy of Nature. This is the zero point, the moment just before the Fool sets out on his journey.

The Fool can appear when you need to get clearer on your purpose before moving forward. This card may also be advising you to stay true to your core self in an uncertain situation. Uncertainty is part of any departure from the status quo, but trusting in your inner sovereignty will help you navigate the unfamiliar territory.

How will the choice you make next ultimately come to affect your circumstances? Sometimes, this is impossible to know. Letting go of thinking you know, or even that you need to know, is a good place to start. At the moment, the only thing you can control is taking the first step. Just be alert to your environment and "look before you leap."

Upright: innocence, a free spirit, spontaneity and beginnings, enthusiasm. Can point to a new job or new relationship, starting over in a new location, or a vacation.

Reversed: recklessness, risk-taking, general foolishness, and naivety. Stay open-minded, but proceed with caution.

I
THE MAGICIAN

The power of intention. Manifestational abilities, readiness, capability, power to create change. The ability to live a magical life is within your grasp.

As the first numbered card of the Major Arcana, the Magician can represent beginnings. But in contrast with the "zero point" of the Fool, the number one indicates that a specific idea or goal is now present. The Fool encounters the Magician first because, having taken the step forward that begins the journey, he has set magical forces in motion. The Magician bridges the ethereal plane with the physical plane, making possible the manifestation of our goals.

This card signifies initiations and acting on one's will, as well as the use of skill, logic, and intellect when taking action. It is also a reminder that the Universe mirrors each of our actions in the greater scheme of things, so we should take care to direct our energy wisely. Keep your focus on desired outcomes, rather than on what has gone wrong or could go wrong.

Upright: skill, concentration, power, action, and resourcefulness. Positive conditions for success in a new endeavor can and should be taken advantage of.

Reversed: hesitation, scattered energy, confusion, poor planning, lack of focus. You may be dealing with a creative block. As a side meaning, the potential for manipulation or trickery.

II
THE HIGH PRIESTESS

Intuition, the divine feminine, mysteries, insights, psychic abilities, spiritual development. The need for careful consideration before acting or making a decision.

The High Priestess signifies wisdom, feminine energy, intuition, the past, secrets, and spirituality. As the second character of the Major Arcana, she often appears when changes are taking place on the inner planes that will be released into outer reality at the appropriate time. As human beings with our own unique pasts, we bring memories and emotional associations to every act and every experience. This card acknowledges the inner forces at work, which may not be consciously known to us, in our responses to external circumstances.

Having set an intention with the Magician phase of the journey, it's now time to consider carefully what the next step is before acting. This card points to the need to listen to and trust your intuition as you proceed down your chosen path.

Upright: insight, clear perception, intuitive revelations, inner knowledge. Be receptive to messages from your higher self at this time. As a side meaning, you may be keeping emotions or secrets to yourself until you know it is safe to reveal them.

Reversed: ignoring intuition, hidden motives, cloudy thinking. There may be hidden agendas on the part of others, or even within your own subconscious. Acting from impulse rather than inner knowing can lead to trouble.

III
THE EMPRESS

Sovereignty, strong feminine energy, beauty, creative force, fertility, rich abundance, nurturing qualities, ability to create change. A favorable time to move forward with your dreams

As the third character of the Fool's Journey, the Empress embodies the creative expression of the inspiration and intuition of the first two cards. She teaches that we are powerful creators who shape our reality through our thoughts, words, and deeds. This card indicates that you are on the right track to make progress, particularly in the areas of abundant growth, harmony in the home, and emotional fulfillment. The Empress also represents sensuality, beauty, and grace and encourages an appreciation of these qualities as you take steps to realize your goals.

As a side meaning, this card may relate to marriage and pregnancy, or the positive influence of a mother figure.

Upright: abundance, fertility, creativity, progress. Your sense of personal sovereignty contributes to your success. A favorable card for issues related to domestic harmony and quality relationships. Stay true to yourself while nurturing others.

Reversed: blocked creativity, unfulfilled potential, insecurity. There is an energy of not believing you can achieve what you desire. Be responsible with money and other forms of abundance, but don't indulge fears about not having enough. May indicate issues with an older woman in your life.

IV
THE EMPEROR

Sovereignty, leadership, strong masculine energy, structure, achievement, responsibility, safety, protection. The power available through discipline and self-control.

As the fourth Major Arcana archetype, the Emperor is associated with construction, formation, and solidity. If the Empress teaches that we are the creators of our reality, the Emperor shows us how to create with intention and discipline. This card often points to the need to build lasting support structures. Structure provides safety and protection, and creates a framework for achieving goals. Overall, the energy of this card is benevolent, representing the universal forces that wish to see you succeed.

As a side meaning, this card may relate to the positive influence of a male leader or father figure, from whom you may wish to seek guidance.

Upright: power, leadership, achievement, stability, protection. Use your personal power, logic, and capacity for self-discipline to bring your goals into being. Energies are favorable for a stable path of progress.

Reversed: domination, inflexibility, excessive control, rigidity. You or someone else may be taking the energy of discipline to an unhealthy or imbalanced extreme. Remember that flexibility is the necessary counterpart to solid structure. You may need to be protective of what you have created.

V
THE HIEROPHANT

Tradition. Wise mentor or leader. Religious or spiritual activity or community. Moral judgement. Conformity to practical approaches or beliefs.

As the fifth archetype of the Major Arcana, this card carries the energies of change and expansion, which are best balanced with tradition and conformity. If the High Priestess points to the inner mystery of our experience, the Hierophant (which means "High Priest" in Greek) points to its outward expression, where we have the opportunity to embody our ethical beliefs. This card reminds us that our journey can be assisted by tradition as we search for truth and understanding. There are benefits to aligning with the wisdom of those who have gone before us.

However, the Hierophant can also point to the need to re-evaluate traditions and communal beliefs in light of new information or experiences. As humanity evolves, so does its collective wisdom and sense of morality. Draw upon your inner wise leader when deciding whether to choose tradition or departure from it. This card often appears when you are on the brink of new spiritual growth.

Upright: practical wisdom, guidance, spiritual progress, ethics. Take advice from someone you trust. You may find, or be, a mentor who can help resolve a challenge.

Reversed: rigid attitudes, dictatorship, manipulation. Someone may be pressuring you to do things their way. You may need to challenge the status quo, at least in your personal belief system.

VI
THE LOVERS

Choices, decisions, relationships, love, friendship, passion, partnership, growth, loyalty. Balancing desires with the needs and wishes of another.

While The Lovers can point to romantic love and sexuality, it is more often associated with the challenges of making choices that involve or affect others, or dealing with choices made by others that affect us. It also points to how our experience of this life is affected by our relationships with others. This card tends to appear when an important decision must be made, often related to the question of our individual values and whether they align with our current circumstances.

As the sixth archetype of the Major Arcana, this card carries the energy of adjustment to new circumstances. As such, the situation indicated by this card might involve sudden changes, or the more gradually dawning understanding that one has outgrown a relationship or an environment.

Upright: love, choices, unions, relationships. Positive alignment between one's beliefs and actions. You are capable of making the right choice. A favorable card in a love or relationship reading.

Reversed: disharmony, fear of commitment, relationship issues. An inability to commit to one choice over another. Disharmony related to relationships or misaligned values. If a breakup is indicated, know that it will ultimately be for the good, even if it doesn't feel that way now.

VII
THE CHARIOT

Victory, achievement, journey, destiny, willpower, determination, self-discipline, control. Harnessing energy to accomplish a goal.

The Chariot archetype speaks to the elements of our life journey that involve determination, forward movement, willpower, and self-control. As the seventh card of the Major Arcana, the Chariot represents the potential to move closer to perfection through spiritual exploration and tempering the ego. Travel in the literal sense may be indicated, but typically this card has more to do with setting out on the road to self-mastery. We are no longer stepping blindly into new adventure, but setting a more determined course.

However, the Chariot also offers a warning, particularly if appearing during times of swift-moving events and high-intensity energy. In the Greek story of Phaeton and the Chariot, young Phaeton's impetuous, over-confident nature causes him to lose control of the chariot that pulls the sun across the sky, ending in global disaster. This card advises us to respect the power of our own will and use it wisely.

Upright: determination, assertion, a drive for adventure. Often a favorable card with regard to journeys or long-term endeavors. Can also point to public recognition for a specific achievement or general success.

Reversed: halted progress, lack of control, impatience. Heading in the wrong direction, the pitfalls of aggression, ego, and arrogance. As a side meaning, can point to travel delays or difficulties.

VIII
JUSTICE

Right action, truth, law, fair decisions, objectivity, discernment, honoring your conscience.

As the eighth card of the Major Arcana, Justice brings the energy of stability and cosmic order. It represents truth, right judgment, resolution, and dealings with the law. Doing what we know is right can be challenging when we are opposed by others. This card may appear when you need to stand up for yourself (provided you are in the right) and for your beliefs.

Justice also teaches us about cause and effect, and the balancing role of karma as a universal principle. It reminds us that actions have consequences. We are impacted by the decisions of others as much as we are by our own. You are advised to pay attention to details in order to come to a balanced and fair conclusion.

At times, this card may appear when you're being too harsh on yourself or others. Remember that Justice isn't about shame or anger—only balance.

Upright: virtue, balance, fair evaluation, right judgement. It's important to remain objective and stay out of ego as you evaluate the situation. Favorable with regard to legal or other decisions not in your control.

Reversed: dishonesty, unfairness, lack of accountability, a moral dilemma. Someone in the situation is behaving dishonorably. The present situation may need to evolve further before a clear understanding of the circumstances can emerge.

IX
THE HERMIT

Retreat, spiritual quest, needing a break from social activity. Following one's own path through inner guidance.

As the ninth archetype of the Major Arcana, the Hermit carries the energies of the mystical three and points to a successful integration of spiritual wisdom. He is a wise figure not only because he has studied and contemplated the mysteries of life, but also because he never stops seeking. As the ninth archetype of the Major Arcana, the Hermit carries the energies of the mystical three and points to a successful integration of spiritual wisdom.

Associated with inner knowledge and self-discovery, this card reminds us that as we seek intellectual and spiritual growth, we have to spend some time in seclusion. You may need to retreat to your inner thoughts to work out how to adapt to new circumstances, or take time and space to process recent developments (whether positive or unwanted).

The Hermit can also indicate a wise mentor, whether you or someone else in your life.

Upright: solitude, inner wisdom, contemplation, going within. A state of solitude and searching, whether in academic study or spiritual pursuits. As a side meaning, the need for recovery after an illness or a harrowing event.

Reversed: loneliness, excessive withdrawal, isolation, confusion. Unpleasant bouts of isolation and loneliness should be tempered with some positive social time with supportive people. You may be ignoring or resisting solid advice from a wise source.

X
THE WHEEL OF FORTUNE

Cycles, turning of events, changing seasons, positive forward motion, the need to stay centered.

The Wheel of Fortune is all about the one constant that we can count on in life—change. As the tenth and final card of the decad within the Major Arcana, it highlights the cyclical energy of the Universe. As events and circumstances come to a close, the stage is set for new developments.

This card often appears in a reading concerning unexpected or unforeseen developments that change your plans or alter your course, for better or worse. Whether you're in advantageous circumstances or in the midst of struggle, know that the Wheel is always turning—the most stable place to be is actually in the center, rather than on top or bottom. In that sense, this card may be advising you not to get attached to particular outcomes at this time. No matter how well we plan or prepare, no one is ever completely in control of events. But this card reminds us that everything—the good and the bad—is temporary.

Upright: positive change, end of delays, a lucky break. A positive turn of events, whether happening presently or somewhere on the horizon. May manifest as a new career opportunity or a financial windfall.

Reversed: instability, unexpected disturbance, short-term success. A temporary downturn in luck due to external forces beyond your control. Be prepared for contingencies. Success that can't last or is built on shaky ground.

XI
STRENGTH

Fortitude, perseverance, inner strength, grace under fire, forgiveness.

Composure and tranquility in adverse situations. The Strength card often appears when we are facing challenges that seem insurmountable, reassuring us that we have what it takes to persevere.

Strength can often be confused with the ability to exert brute force, but as a virtue, strength harnesses the powers of patience and love and actually tames the energies of anger and ferocity. You are being encouraged to exert control over your life through love and confidence rather than force.

This card also acknowledges that we struggle, as imperfect beings, with desires and instincts that may not always be best to pursue. Here, will-power and determination are required to in order to follow the path of our highest good. Powerful spiritual forces may be at work in your life at this time.

Upright: compassion, endurance, patience, courage, self-confidence. You have all you need inside you to weather any present storm. As a side meaning, can also indicate good health.

Reversed: self-doubt, lack of self-discipline, weakness. Resist the urge to act out of anger, frustration, or fear. Avoiding conflicts or confrontations will only make a problem worse in the long run. It may be time to face an unhealthy or addictive behavior.

XII
THE HANGED MAN

Time of wait, needing a rest, things at a standstill. The need for a new perspective. Opportunity for inner peace.

The Hanged Man is considered one of the most important Tarot archetypes in the journey of the soul. This card is not about being persecuted or punished—rather, it reminds us that great insights often follow periods of great difficulty, and that there is value in "down time." It teaches patience and the value of right timing.

This card may appear when you're feeling overwhelmed by circumstances and can't see a way forward. Or, the way forward may be temporarily blocked. This card advises that there's no point in straining or struggling against current obstacles at this time. Trust that things are being worked out behind the scenes and relax for now.

The Hanged Man represents the opportunity to gain a fresh perspective, but only after spending some time in stillness, and perhaps letting go of old plans or dreams. Focus on the present for now, rather than dwelling on the past or worrying about what happens next.

Upright: waiting, temporary pause, letting go, meditation. The need for a time out. Embrace the stillness. Identify what you need for the next stage of your journey before moving forward.

Reversed: fear of change, time to act, missed opportunities. Let go of old ideas so you can be open to new understanding. Don't sell yourself short in order to stay in your comfort zone.

XIII
DEATH

Endings, new beginnings, renewal, change, transformation, turning point, clearing.

The Death card is almost never about literal physical death. Instead, this card may appear in a reading when a situation is naturally ending, whether it's a relationship, a job, or even an era in one's life. You are advised to let go of what is no longer serving you, the way a tree will shed its leaves to make room for new growth when the seasons turn. Another appropriate symbol for this card is the mythical Phoenix, who cyclically rises from the ashes of its own demise. This card follows The Hanged Man as the soul learns to let go of the old in preparation for the new.

This card can also signify the resolution of old conflicts or issues. You may be undergoing a transformative cleansing of outdated beliefs or stale dreams. New blessings will soon arrive to fill the space you are currently clearing out.

Upright: endings, change, transition, new beginnings, transformation. A clean sweep. The clearing out of the old. You will soon see that this change is for the better.

Reversed: stagnation, stuck energy, defeat. Inability to move on from a situation due to a fierce resistance to change. Take steps to release what has ended so that new opportunities can take root.

XIV
TEMPERANCE

Balance, moderation, compromise, fusion, teamwork, connectedness.

The Temperance card represents the needs that arise as we work to incorporate new ideas, information, circumstances, and/or spiritual growth into our daily lives. Having experienced extremes of all kinds along our journey, especially in the realms of emotion and attitudes, we eventually come to value balance. Temperance mixes the inner world of the psyche with the external physical world, and this card often appears in the context of seeking to bring an ideal into reality.

Temperance reminds us that synchronicity of timing is available to all, as long as we are still and balanced enough to recognize it. It also helps us appreciate the interconnectedness of all things. Cooperation, both with universal forces and with other people, can lead to great progress in a relationship, business, or project. If you are feeling pulled in several opposing directions, take a break and ask for guidance. Temperance is the key to keeping positive influences in forward motion.

<u>Upright:</u> communication, good timing, balance, equanimity. Be patient with yourself and others. Use your diplomacy skills to help resolve a conflict.

<u>Reversed:</u> imbalance, a lack of long term vision, impatience, tendency toward excess. Do what you can to balance your responses to external issues in a healthy way. If money problems are involved, deal with them responsibly before they get worse.

XV
THE DEVIL

Choices and consequences. Fear or worry. Materialism. A sense of feeling trapped. Liberation versus restriction.

The Devil does not represent the evil figure of the Christian worldview. Instead, this card speaks to the inner wildness we all possess that generally needs some management, through the skills associated with cards like Temperance, the Hermit, and Justice. Our primal nature is not something to be suppressed, but rather judiciously drawn from as we navigate our lives within society. We have free will to choose well.

This card may indicate that you've allowed your ego to make you feel separate from the interconnectedness of the Universe, perhaps by focusing on fear and negativity. Sometimes too much focus on the material world can make us lose perspective. The Devil may also point to addictive behaviors that are holding you back, which you may or may not be conscious of.

On the other hand, this card may indicate that you're neglecting your inner wild side too much. If you have too tight a reign on your behavior, you may be starving your creative powers, so trust yourself and let loose a little.

Upright: short-sightedness, impulsivity, choices, liberation over restriction. Examine your motives carefully with regard to your current circumstances. Keep the bigger picture in mind.

Reversed: imprisonment, selfishness, obsession, inhibitions. You may be restricting yourself unnecessarily. Fear of lack or fear of being judged. May also indicate a struggle with a problematic addiction.

XVI
THE TOWER

Sudden changes, revelations, chaos, destruction, transformation. A major life event.

The Tower card signals transformation, the shattering of illusion, and sudden change. It often arises in situations that affect a group or community, but can also point to a a personal event for you or someone close to you. Previously unknown truths may be revealed, which could be unpleasant but need to be known so that a situation can be resolved.

This energy is abrupt and may be unsettling or even frightening. It may mark the loss of a position or some other change with enormous implications. This event can be a result of the Universe "course-correcting" when you need a shake-up in order to get back on the path to your highest ideals. If you sense this is the case, take it as a positive, loving push in the right direction.

The Tower doesn't always indicate a literal event, however. The spiritual meaning in this card is in the shattering of old constructs as the light of truth and higher consciousness prevails.

Upright: temporary chaos, revelations, transformation, unexpected change. Turbulence that leads to beneficial outcomes. You will gain new wisdom from the situation, which you can use in the future.

Reversed: stale or stagnant energy, ignoring reality, unsustainable pressure. Resistance, fear of change, dishonesty, or willful blindness may be aggravating a situation or placing you at risk of losing everything.

XVII
THE STAR

Harmony, optimism, hope, creative power, alignment, good luck. Moving in the right direction.

The Star appears in the Fool's journey as the calm after the storm, which was kicked up in the events of The Tower card. It is also a reward for the changes in perspective and releasing of old patterns that several prior cards in the Major Arcana have advised. After chaos, disillusionment, and letting go, new clarity arises. While the significance of this card in a reading may relate to past events, the focus is on the future, and faith in the journey as we awaken to the larger patterns of meaning in the Universe.

The energy of the Star card can point to sudden breakthroughs or opportunities that seem to come out of the blue. You have "star power" at the moment and can achieve whatever you put your effort into. However, this energetic alignment isn't permanent, so don't procrastinate. This card advises you to take the next step as soon as possible.

Upright: inspiration, good prospects, positive change, new ideas, rewards. Alignment with the source of creation. You are on the right path and able to use your creativity to manifest your desires.

Reversed: discouragement, despair, lack of faith, blocked creativity. A project or relationship may be losing steam. Get back in touch with your inner guidance, and ask for help from those you trust.

XVIII
THE MOON

Intuition, secrets, psychic abilities, hidden information, dreams. Seeking answers from the unseen realms.

The Moon is one of the more mysterious cards of the Major Arcana, as it deals with psychic knowing as well as illusion. The Moon relates to the collective unconscious, as well as our dreams and intuition. The physical moon provides light reflected from the sun, but this light can only partially illuminate our path, leaving much of the Earth in shadow.

This card may come up to remind us that just as people can be physically and emotionally affected by the energies of the full moon, we are subject to invisible forces that we can only partially sense. You may be navigating a situation with many unseen elements, including secrets or hidden motives on the part of others.

Pay attention to your dreams, as well as any signs and signals in the exterior world that resonate with you, and be patient as you seek clarity. It may not yet be time to act, but closely examine your options, and honor your intuition as you wait for further information. As a side meaning, this card can indicate journeys, whether literal or internal.

Upright: dreams, visions, mystery, trusting intuition. Look beyond surface appearances. Epiphanies through intuition or divine communication.

Reversed: dishonesty, deceit, suspicion, illusion. Mistrusting your own intuition. There may be too much psychic debris in the air to see anything clearly at this time.

XIX
THE SUN

Happiness, joy, success, positive outcomes, self-confidence, new ideas, security, gratitude, well-being. Very favorable circumstances. Everything falls into place.

The Sun is the card of enlightenment, achievement, victory, and joy. It represents the dawn of a new day after the worst and darkest night. The Sun is the source of life, growth, and optimism. With this energy, we are granted time to bask in the successes of our journey thus far and enjoy good times with family and community. This card is not so much about swift forward movement as it is a moment to appreciate where you are. It's important to appreciate times of rest and feelings of security.

The Sun is also associated with the dawn of the inner light of each soul on the spiritual quest. This card may indicate new ideas that lead to ingenious solutions. It is said that this card has no truly severe indications--all is well, or soon will be, when the Sun appears. If you're not feeling this now, remember that the sun always returns from behind the clouds, so be patient and hang in there.

Upright: positivity, success, fun, warmth, harmony contentment. A period of joy and security. All is well.

Reversed: setback, delay, insecurity, temporary blues. Don't focus on what isn't working right now. Trust that the experiences of joy, success, and easy rest will come again.

XX
JUDGMENT

Evaluation, self-assessment, reviewing past choices, harvest, renewal.

Judgment is associated with truth, renewal, forgiveness, freedom, and higher consciousness.

In the context of the Fool's Journey, the Judgment card appears when it's time to review prior experiences, examine what we've learned, and make decisions about how best to move forward. Evaluating our prior beliefs in light of what we've recently experienced can bring about new insight, and help us better understand our past. This card may also indicate a conflict between one's personal experiences and beliefs and the dominant attitudes of one's community or society in general.

Judgment is also about reaping the rewards of past efforts as well as the consequences of past actions. You may be being asked to forgive yourself or others for wrongdoings in order to make space for new spiritual or emotional growth. If there are amends to be made, now is the time. Absolution and renewal can only occur after you let go.

Upright: rebirth, rewards, forgiveness, reckoning. Rewards for past efforts that will help your future success. Making wise changes.

Reversed: regret, grudges, unwanted consequences from past choices.You may be refusing to examine your own role in your circumstances. Alternatively, others may be judging you unfairly and you may not know how to stand up for yourself.

XXI
THE WORLD

Completion, journey's end, success, celebration, achievement, triumph, reward, wholeness.

The World card appears at the triumphant conclusion of the Fool's Journey. After many adventures, trials, missteps, and revelations, the soul has reached its sought-after destination. This is a fortuitous card with an energy of peace, satisfaction, success, and being fully in touch with one's true self. Of course, the spiritual journey is always cyclical, so there will soon be a new starting point for the soul to embark from. But for now, it is time to enjoy a moment of completion.

Whether your question is about relationships, career, health, or a spiritual quest, this card represents the achievement of the goal. Celebrate your capacity for manifesting desired results within your reality.

As a side meaning, you may be in position to embark on a physical journey, whether for work or leisure.

Upright: joy, accomplishment, objectives met. A cause for celebration. Possible material gains. A goal has been achieved or a difficult dilemma has been resolved. The way is now paved for new beginnings.

Reversed: lack of closure, incomplete results, unresolved situation. More work to be done. Alternatively, you may be trying too hard to achieve results before circumstances are favorable for doing so.

THE CARDS OF THE
MINOR ARCANA

THE SUIT OF WANDS

Wands represent the "spark" of inspiration that is transformed into action and manifestation. Wands symbolize a desire to grow, expand, create, and take risks in order to make things happen.

If many Wands appear in a reading, this is an indication that things are either just beginning, or are still in the realm of ideas, not yet manifest. Wands also point to what we desire and what we fear, since these two feelings are usually the source of our motivations.

Key words used often in association with Wands: new ideas, ambition, new ventures, inspiration, enthusiasm, growth, expansion.

ACE OF WANDS

Upright: inspiration, potential, new beginnings, creative success

Powerful inspiration. An idea you feel strongly about. Success in all kinds of new plans & projects. Energy moving upward and outward with force and enthusiasm, often related to career or a creative pursuit. This is a good time to take an important step forward.

Reversed: lack of motion, lack of inspiration, delays

Feeling uninspired or losing enthusiasm for an endeavor. Frustration due to delayed projects or activities, possibly due to lack of sufficient planning. Inability to move forward. Timing for acting on ideas or starting new projects is momentarily unfavorable, but with patience, success is still within reach.

TWO OF WANDS

Upright: progress, planning the future, discovery, decisions, a reliable partner

Making future plans from a stable and optimistic vantage point. Assistance and progress in career endeavors. An equal partnership. New discoveries will be encouraging. Efforts already undertaken will be worthwhile.

Reversed: lack of planning, fear of the unknown, inequality

Lack of effective planning or fear of moving forward. Difficulty making a decision. An unequal partnership in terms of influence, input, or financial resources. An imbalance of work load (real or perceived), or dissatisfaction with progress made thus far.

THREE OF WANDS

Upright: expansion, foresight, cooperation, creativity, success

Initiative pays off. Good returns on a venture. Your efforts are working, particularly when they involve creative approaches to solving problems. Optimism is justified. In the development of projects, events speed up. Cooperation and assistance from others are part of the equation. A good time for making or adjusting long-term plans.

Reversed: delays, lack of foresight, obstacles, misconceptions

Lack of planning or faulty planning. Lack of cooperation from or with others. Progress halted due to stubbornness or outdated ideas. Misunderstandings between people (usually groups of at least three). Stay as neutral as you can and avoid direct confrontations during this time.

FOUR OF WANDS

Upright: harmony, stability, attainment, contentment, teamwork

Satisfaction and harmony. Steady abundance. Enjoying the rewards of your efforts thus far, whether in work or creative pursuits. Productive collaboration with others. A feeling of celebration and knowing that all is well. Sometimes indicates romance or marriage.

Reversed: delays, disorganization, dissatisfaction

Dissatisfaction with the results of your efforts. Feeling success is always just out of reach. An unfinished project is at a standstill, possibly due to someone not pulling their weight. Stay focused on the actions you can take and take your attention away from what's not working. What you resist persists.

FIVE OF WANDS

Upright: competition, disagreement, teamwork, diligence, struggle to coordinate

Cooperation is a challenge but needed at this time. Feeling at odds with others, particularly in a work or collaborative situation. Competing desires or opinions. The need to regroup or get on the same page with others. Imbalance between ambition and waiting for right timing. Pay attention to details and don't give up. Discomfort caused by chaos leads to growth.

Reversed: tension, strife, conflict, stubbornness

A more intense form of the upright position. Dealing with strong opposition or stubbornness in a group situation. A complex dispute. Being on the receiving end of unfair judgments or the results of a shake-up of normal circumstances. The need to accept that another person won't change their mind, no matter what. Stay out of resentment as much as you can--it doesn't help move things forward.

SIX OF WANDS

Upright: victory, success, public recognition, self-confidence, progress, reward

Well-earned victory after much effort and overcoming obstacles. Good news, success and completion of tasks at hand. Moving forward after being temporarily stalled. Possible awards or other public recognition for your achievements. A good time for resolving legal matters, delayed contracts, or a work issue. You succeed, and your reward is well deserved.

Reversed: disappointment, egotism, lack of confidence

Lack of success, possibly due to overestimating abilities. Feeling undervalued or deserving of recognition that hasn't come. Insecurity. General delays to plans. Complex and entrenched obstacles. The need to identify blind spots and regroup before making further attempts.

SEVEN OF WANDS

Upright: competition, overcoming challenge, defensive advantage, self-confidence, strength

A person or situation is stirring up dynamic energy. An advantage over adversaries. Being challenged or opposed by others, but having the necessary experience and abilities to emerge victorious. Standing up for oneself and one's beliefs. Choosing battles wisely. Ability to beat the odds. Success despite criticism or opposition.

Reversed: stalemate, overwhelm, self-doubt, resistance, surrender

A stalemate in a situation involving communications or negotiations with others. Being unheard or overruled in a group dispute. Doubting one's abilities to persevere. Digging in to an argument that can't be resolved. The need to discern whether perseverance is warranted when it might be better in the long run to walk away.

EIGHT OF WANDS

Upright: changes, travel, swift movement, opportunities, multitasking

A period of many developments unfolding at once. Forward movement after a period of waiting. Sudden progress toward attainment of a goal. Having many plates spinning at once. The need for multitasking. The arrival of important news. As a side meaning, a journey may be involved.

Reversed: overwhelm, destabilization, delays, sluggish progress, discernment

Overwhelm due to too much happening at once. Being caught off-guard by sudden changes or fast-moving events. Unexpected delays. Uncertainty about potential opportunities. Avoid making hasty decisions just to solve problems quickly—waiting is more advantageous at this time.

NINE OF WANDS

Upright: assistance, persistence, courage, vigilance, resourcefulness

Plans are on the verge of being realized. An impending boost of assistance to reach completion. The need to realize that this support is available. Feeling the need to protect one's plans, progress, or creations. Anticipating and being prepared for difficulties. Being vigilant and determined. Direct your energy toward practical considerations rather than fears about unknowns.

Reversed: defensiveness, suspicion, threats, lack of persistence

Being too defensive or suspicious of others, possibly to an extreme of paranoia. Past negative experiences may be coloring your sense of the present. Perspective lost due to some kind of trauma. Immobilization due to unwarranted mistrust. Possible threats to stability in a career or business situation. Lack of energy or motivation to continue with plans, despite progress made so far.

TEN OF WANDS

Upright: a burden, too much work, imbalance, determination, achievement

A tendency toward workaholism. An imbalance between work and leisure. Making things harder than they need to be. Micromanaging and doing others' work for them unnecessarily. The need to delegate and/or ask for assistance. Strong determination and a desire for success on one's own terms. Self-assured and capable but sometimes to a fault. Early in a reading, this card signals that clear answers may not be available right now.

Reversed: overwhelm, burnout, blame, self-deception

A more severe form of the upright position. Inability to proceed due to total burnout. Taking on more than you can handle but blaming others for your decisions. Indulging in martyrdom mentality. Take responsibility for your part in this situation, and identify what you can do differently from now on. New levels of success always require strategic adjustments.

PAGE OF WANDS

Upright: optimism, enthusiasm, discovery, ambition, caution

Having a lot of enthusiasm and being energized for the task at hand. Good news about a new opportunity or a current venture. Potentially seeking guidance about optimal next steps. An outgoing or optimistic person. One who demonstrates resourcefulness, creativity, and an enterprising spirit. The need to beware of unbridled enthusiasm without follow-through. Check in with yourself and investigate opportunities thoroughly before committing.

Reversed: pessimism, pettiness, setbacks, manipulation, lack of direction, gossip

Inability to find passion for a worthwhile goal. Healthy skepticism about opportunities becomes pessimism to an immobilizing extent. A person who demonstrates shallow-mindedness and/or enjoys stirring things up. Being flighty. Gossip or malicious talk may be circulating. Resist any temptation to join in.

KNIGHT OF WANDS

Upright: enthusiasm, passion, energy, restlessness, adventure

Forward movement. A possible new career venture. Seeking out new opportunities with energy and enthusiasm. Taking plans, skills, or experiences to a new level. Immediate action, often necessitated by a sudden change. A charming, adventurous, forward-looking and even daring person. A possible tendency toward restlessness or premature action.

Reversed: scattered energy, impulsiveness, frustration, delays, insincerity

Energy for forward movement but no solid results yet, particularly related to job-seeking. Anxiousness to get started on something, perhaps before all is ready to go. Be sure to pay attention to details at this time. Someone who comes on too strong, whether romantically, in business, or in a family dynamic.

QUEEN OF WANDS

Upright: accomplishment, vibrance, self-mastery, inspiration, optimism

The accomplishment of a long-held or long-term goal. A highly charged creative energy. A vibrant and inspiring presence. A person who is practical, talented, and confident. One who demonstrates the qualities of kindness, loyalty, dependability, warmth, and/or optimism. Someone who can offer good advice.

Reversed: neglect, unreliability, disinterest, criticism

A project or goal is derailed by a lack of promised support. A lack of practicality. Disinterest in one's current tasks. A person who criticizes from meanness rather than a desire to help. Jealousy over the success of others.

KING OF WANDS

Upright: satisfaction, wisdom, vision, leadership, honor, compassion

An energy of satisfaction with progress and accomplishments. Someone who can give advice from the benefit of experience. A person demonstrating the qualities of trustworthiness, wisdom, and honesty. A natural leader who can inspire and motivate others and takes an innovative approach. Possibly a father figure.

Reversed: negativity, control, thoughtlessness

An energy of intolerance and narrow-mindedness. Negative thoughts and attitudes. There may be difficult negotiations or deliberations at this time. Someone who behaves in a domineering or controlling manner. Dismissing the efforts of others. A tendency to stifle creativity.

THE SUIT OF CUPS

Cups represent love, relationships, emotions, creativity, intuition, and imagination. When we respond emotionally to ideas, events, and environments, we are in the energetic realm of Cups.

Many Cups in a reading can signal that the main forces at play in our current circumstances are rooted in emotion or intuition. These cards speak to matters of the heart and/or psychic receptivity, and may point to a need to open up to others or to establish useful boundaries.

Key words used often in association with Cups: emotion, desire, inner experience, relationships, intuition, creativity.

ACE OF CUPS

Upright: love, new emotional experience, creativity, psychic abilities

Potential for emotional fulfillment and contentment. A fresh start, possibly in the form of a new love relationship or in healing from past heartbreak. Bliss. Advises receptivity to new emotions and new connections with others in romance and/or friendship. Also speaks to psychic/astral connections and a new flow of creativity— potential in these areas awaits your willingness to be receptive. Pregnancy or childbirth may also be indicated.

Reversed: repressed or blocked emotions, creative stagnation

An emotional block may prevent the growth of love, leading to stagnation and emptiness. Anxiety around having enough time or emotional energy to spend with loved ones. Possibly a warning about being too psychically open and the need to establish energetic boundaries. Problems with fertility may also be indicated.

TWO OF CUPS

Upright: joy, partnership, relationships, communication, harmony

A joyful, emotionally rewarding partnership is growing, whether in romance, friendship, work, or business. An easy flow of creativity and good communication. May indicate an engagement or other happy agreement between two people. Also points to the benefits of forgiveness as a means of moving forward into harmony. Inner emotional balance and sense of well-being.

Reversed: disharmony, relationship imbalance, separation, miscommunication

In a partnership, one person may be unwilling to commit. Communication failures lead to jealousy or other divisions. An inability to forgive or make amends. Being at odds with one's own feelings.

THREE OF CUPS

Upright: friendship, celebrations, community, creativity, growth, healing

A period of happiness and celebration. Feeling rejuvenated, physically and emotionally. Positive outcomes to a situation, especially regarding healing from illness or injury. Creativity flourishes. Mutual support within a group of friends or family. Childbirth may be indicated or new projects may be taking shape.

Reversed: creative blocks, isolation, betrayal

Feeling left out or unappreciated. Separation from friends or family due to emotional conflict. Disappointment with current outlook and blocked creativity. Low energy and possible health problems. Feeling cut off from the happiness of others.

FOUR OF CUPS

Upright: contemplation, reevaluation, boredom, distraction, opportunity for clarity

A point where past contentment gives way to wanting something more. Material needs are met, but emotional or creative needs are asking for attention. Monotony may begin to manifest in a relationship, spurring a reassessment. You may be distracted or preoccupied and therefore missing opportunities or messages the Universe is sending your way.

Reversed: apathy, numbness, depression, avoidance

A more severe form of the upright position. A time of apathy and fatigue, where nothing is fulfilling. Emotional burnout, feeling isolated and/or depressed. May also indicate poor physical health. A relationship may be static or even stifling. Refusing to acknowledge an issue, staying distracted to avoid self-reflection. Take interest in something creative, no matter how seemingly insignificant, to help break up the stagnant energy.

FIVE OF CUPS

Upright: disappointment, loss, inability to move on, regret, unhappiness

The need to release old emotions and find new perspective. Feeling let down by circumstances. Inability to focus on positive feelings, dwelling on past disappointments or losses. This may relate to unhappy relationships, whether romantic love or friendship, or regrets over past behavior. Removing yourself from negative situations or people. Dwelling on what has gone wrong blocks you from new opportunities. Be patient and focus on what is going well. As a side meaning, issues with an inheritance may be involved.

Reversed: acceptance, moving on, forgiveness, healing, hope

Emotional wounds are healing. Your ability to let go of old disappointments makes room for new, positive developments to come into your life. Forgiving past hurts or injustices. Forgiving yourself. Making needed changes and moving forward with optimism.

SIX OF CUPS

Upright: happiness, reunions, the past, nostalgia, childhood, benefits of experience

The past as a positive influence. Old friends, acquaintances, or romantic partners return, usually briefly. Fond reminiscences. An appreciation for all you've learned from past experiences, both joyful and challenging. Reconnecting with your inner childlike sense of wonder. Matters involving children or childhood.

Reversed: melancholy, being stuck in the past, being unrealistic, sentimentality

Misremembering or over-sentimentalizing the past. Being stuck in the past and unable to accept present circumstances. Inability to take advantage of the chance to develop new relationships. A partnership, romantic or otherwise, that seems to have no future.

SEVEN OF CUPS

Upright: choices, opportunities, uncertainty, wishful thinking

Uncertainty about which of many possible directions to choose. Many opportunities or invitations arise, possibly in love relationships or creative endeavors. Some have a lot of potential, while others may be too good to be true. The need to avoid making unwise decisions based on unrealistic expectations. The need to integrate heart, intuition, and mind to make the best choice.

Reversed: indecision, confusion, self-deception, fantasy, avoidance

Overwhelm, indecision, or anxiety about having too many options. Being too attached to a particular relationship, situation, or idea to acknowledge issues or problems. False promises. A disconnect between heart and mind. Trying to escape into fantasies or false realities to avoid making a difficult choice. Ignoring intuition.

EIGHT OF CUPS

Upright: turning point, contemplation, seeking meaning, moving on

The decision to make a change for the better. Leaving something behind, whether a job, a home, a relationship, or an old habit of thought or behavior. A choice to move on may be spurred by disappointments or defeats, but still facilitates positive growth. Contemplation and seeking perspective. The desire for a more spiritually fulfilling life. Spending time in nature can help you gain emotional clarity.

Reversed: abandonment, disappointment, unwanted change, hopelessness, poor judgement

Deep disappointment about the end of a relationship or career situation. Feeling abandoned by someone, or let down by circumstances beyond your control. Dwelling on the unfortunate turn of events can blind you to positive opportunities. Choosing to stay in unhealthy situations or behaviors rather than face the discomfort of change.

NINE OF CUPS

Upright: wishes fulfilled, happiness, comfort, satisfying relationships

Wishes come true. Happiness and contentment are dominant now. End of concerns or emotional difficulty. Psychic intuitive abilities are enhanced. Good news, good health, and emotional fulfillment, particularly in relationships. A feeling of magic in the air. Know that these energies are there, even if you can't feel them right this minute. Focusing on the positive brings what you want into your life, especially at this time.

Reversed: dissatisfaction, greed, selfishness, irresponsibility

A warning against indulging selfishness, greed, or pride. Egotism wreaks havoc on love relationships or friendships, resulting in emotional wounding and disharmony. Focusing too much on self-interests at the expense of others. Irresponsibility and poor choices lead to dissatisfaction with outcomes. Feeling that desires will never materialize.

TEN OF CUPS

Upright: love, joy, happiness, contentment, family, security, harmony

The feeling of living a purposeful life. Self-esteem and a sense of connectedness. Healthy and fulfilling relationships in romance, friendship, and/or the family. Emotional support and well-being. Stability, especially within the home. Enjoyment, satisfaction, and a feeling of wholeness. Relationships and group activities are peaceful and harmonious. Occasions for reunion. A possible marriage or a child on the way.

Reversed: disruption, disharmony, family quarrels, instability

Temporary disharmony or instability arises in a family or other group. An interruption of an otherwise-peaceful time. A relationship breaks down. Feeling lonely or isolated or being away from family. An unfavorable time for group activities or events. Looking for emotional support in the wrong places. The need to derive self-esteem or self-worth from within, as opposed to from others.

PAGE OF CUPS

Upright: creativity, guidance, friendship, romance, connection

Good news about a relationship, potentially a new romance or friendship. A trustworthy and understanding friend. Seeking or providing guidance on an emotional issue. The need for a creative outlet, possibly for healing purposes. Talent and appreciation for art. A youthful energy that favors creative expression and heightened intuitive abilities. A person who is creative, emotionally sensitive, and a bit mystical. Possibly a message via a dream or divination.

Reversed: creative block, emotional immaturity, frustration

A personality that has trouble with positive self-expression. Inability to tap into inner creativity. An energy of immaturity, possibly via a child or adolescent who is seeking attention. A dreamy and unfocused energy. A possible need to be more grounded in approach to romantic love.

KNIGHT OF CUPS

Upright: romance, flirtation, affection, strong emotions, dreaminess, inspiration

A strong rush of feelings, often unexpected. An intense emotional experience. Can indicate a new, sudden romance or someone with something beneficial to offer. An increase in creative energy and inspiration. A celebratory energy that encourages sociability and gratitude for good times. A person who is flirtatious, passionate, dreamy, and even dramatic. Relationships begun under this influence can be very passionate and enjoyable, but may not last long.

Reversed: impracticality, moodiness, insincerity, deception, emptiness

Emotional upheaval due to sudden events or to not being sufficiently grounded in reality. An energy of broken promises and deceit. A person whose words should be taken with a giant grain of salt, even if they appear to be flattering. Possible regret over a passionate affair that turned out to be empty of true feelings.

QUEEN OF CUPS

Upright: compassion, intuition, emotional intelligence

Strong psychic connections, possibly to a specific person. A period of psychic tides washing in. A person with patience, empathy, and intuition, who is comfortable in the realm of emotion. A natural caregiver with mature, maternal energy. Someone who demonstrates loving, nurturing, and/or romantic qualities. Considering the needs of the family and/or community when making plans.

Reversed: emotional insecurity, moodiness, co-dependency, overwhelm

Putting others first to a self-defeating or unhealthy degree, perhaps to distract from one's own issues. Being overwhelmed by feelings, emotions, and/or psychic impressions. Over-romanticizing a situation rather than looking at it critically. Someone who is emotionally needy and energetically draining.

KING OF CUPS

<u>Upright:</u> enjoyment, blessings, compassion, advice, emotional balance, spirituality

Blessings and good feelings abound. A general and consistent feeling that all is well. A cause for major celebration. A benevolent influence, possibly in the form of a wise, compassionate counselor or healer. Someone who can offer heart-centered advice. A person who demonstrates the qualities of honor, devotion, warmth, and/or compassion. A loyal, reliable, and considerate person. Gaining mastery of spiritual awareness and connection.

<u>Reversed:</u> numbness, spiritual isolation, corruption, ego, emotional manipulation, volatility

Being closed off to one's feelings and to spiritual connection. The potential for corruption. Advice based on ego rather than the heart. An emotionally inconsistent or manipulative person. The potential for destructive behavior.

THE SUIT OF SWORDS

Swords represent action, movement, and the means through which ideas are brought forth into physical reality. Swords are logical rather than emotional, and are seen symbolically as cutting through illusion and sharpening the intellect. They advise approaching problems by using reason rather than focusing on feelings.

Many Swords in a reading may reflect a high level of activity or commotion in a current situation as it moves toward a final result, and/or indicate a need for careful consideration before making a move.

Key words used often in association with Swords: action, movement, struggle, conflict, strategy, responsibility, clarity.

ACE OF SWORDS

Upright: victory, progress, mental clarity, break-throughs, justice

Potential for action, breakthroughs, clarity, achievement. A strong level of activity that will lead to success. Intellectual ability. You have the clarity of mind to make sound decisions about what step to take next. Focused action is needed to withstand challenges, but victory and progress prevail over obstacles. A fair resolution to a conflict.

Reversed: stagnation, lack of clarity, unfair dealings

Failure or frustration about lack of motion. Delayed action. Confusion or cloudy thinking. Mental exhaustion. Dwelling too much on what's not working keeps you from seeing possible solutions. Take a break from the issue rather than spinning your wheels. Potential for dishonesty or unfair dealings.

TWO OF SWORDS

<u>Upright:</u> choices, indecision, stalemate, truce

Competition between people, egos, or ideas. Inability to make a decision. The need for negotiation and compromise, regardless of feelings. Objectivity is especially important now—be willing to balance your needs with those of the other person or people involved. There is much potential for conflicts to be resolved.

<u>Reversed:</u> confusion, suspicion, betrayal, suspicion

Lack of trust, possibly stemming from deception in a partnership. An atmosphere of drama and manipulation as opposed to straightforward dealings. Unwillingness to compromise. Doubt over prior decisions and giving into fear.

THREE OF SWORDS

<u>Upright:</u> sorrow, disappointment, resignation, perseverance

Disillusionment and even grief caused by unwanted outcomes. A need to reassess based on unexpected and unpleasant developments. Dealing with the unknown. The need to avoid becoming trapped by negative thinking. Accept the situation, knowing that something better will emerge in place of what was lost, and keep putting one foot in front of the other.

<u>Reversed:</u> struggle, confusion, chaos

Drama and upheaval. Chaos as a result of unexpected events. Being immobilized by indecision or fear of making mistakes. Struggling to get out of a relationship or commitment that has turned out other than expected.

FOUR OF SWORDS

<u>Upright:</u> recovery, contemplation, relaxation, vacation, rest

A period of calm and recovery after a time of intense activity and/or pressure. The need to take time out before making a big decision or trying to solve a problem. Distance is needed from a challenging situation so it can be objectively analyzed. Taking a break from the usual routine in order to recharge. Recuperation from illness may also be indicated.

<u>Reversed:</u> illness, disruption, burnout, hyper-vigilance, avoidance

Illness or some other unexpected development may be requiring you to take time off from normal daily life. Feeling isolated from others for circumstantial reasons. Feeling burned out on an endeavor. Possible restlessness or insomnia. The tendency to keep your guard up when it isn't necessary. May also indicate a tendency to set problems aside in order to avoid dealing with them.

FIVE OF SWORDS

<u>Upright:</u> tension, conflict, defeat, change in perspective, moment of truth

A wake-up call. Swift change in perspective based on new revelations. The need to accept that a current problem or conflict doesn't have a satisfactory solution. You may need to cut your losses and move on. The opportunity to learn from defeat. The need for courage and self-confidence in the face of adversity. Choose your battles wisely.

<u>Reversed:</u> willful blindness, ego domination, betrayal, stagnation

Digging into conflict out of fear of admitting being wrong. Wanting to win at all costs. Listening to the ego rather than the rational mind. Fear of criticism. Someone in a conflict may be engaged in betrayal, whether of others or of themself. The inability to make progress due to fear of defeat.

SIX OF SWORDS

Upright: improvement, end of difficulties, peace restored, a necessary transition, a journey

After possibly a long period of difficulty, harmony is restored. Things may not be completed, but steady progress is now being made. Ability to cut one's losses in order to move into better circumstances. Leaving troubles behind, possibly through changing jobs or relocating. An upcoming journey of some kind.

Reversed: turbulence, enforced change, dwelling on loss, upheaval

A change in circumstances beyond one's control, possibly leading to disorientation or turmoil. Exhaustion from continued struggle. Improvements are delayed, or go unrecognized due to focusing on recent losses. Being forced to relocate or find a new job when unprepared to do so.

SEVEN OF SWORDS

Upright: clarity, strategy, self-confidence, cunning, stealth

Searching for the truth about a situation. Seeking or receiving clarity. A new development may require an adjusted strategy, but clever planning paves the way to overcome obstacles or opposition. Maintain civility and self-confidence in a dispute but be on the lookout for dishonesty. It may be wise to keep your plans and your resources to yourself at this time.

Reversed: confusion, secrets, betrayal, timidity, indecision

Inability to see a clear path or next step, possibly due to hidden agendas on the part of others. Someone may be trying to force a decision due to self-interest. Listening to your intuition is crucial now. The potential for theft, deception, or other betrayals. Don't allow anyone to convince you to do anything that you don't resonate with completely. Be courageous in standing your ground.

EIGHT OF SWORDS

Upright: blind trust, patience, healing, right timing, constraint

The need to trust in right timing and stay the course. Outcomes or answers are still hidden from view. The need for patience, possibly relating to recuperating from illness or injury. Feeling trapped by current circumstances. Don't push things too fast or make a hasty decision that's out of alignment with your long-term good.

Reversed: doubt, pessimism, self-imposed restriction, self-blame

Trapped by negative thinking and a tendency to expect the worst. Allowing doubt to prevent action toward progress. Regrets about jumping to conclusions or premature actions. Being too caught up in guilt and self-reproach to see a way out of the problem. The need for self-forgiveness.

NINE OF SWORDS

Upright: anxiety, stress, unwarranted fears, nightmares

A battle within the mind between objectivity and fear. Fears are unwarranted or at the very least exaggerated with respect to the actual problem. Expecting terrible outcomes. Troubled thoughts and possibly lost sleep or nightmares. Do what you can to take your mind off of the problem for now. Get some fresh perspective so you can take proactive steps with confidence.

Reversed: hopelessness, torment, victimization, fears realized

A more extreme form of the upright position. Being so full of fear or despair that no positive thoughts are possible. Being attached to a victim role. A fixation on a negative outcome may have actually helped to bring it into being. Don't compound it by continuing to focus on the problem. Acknowledge that the "other shoe" has dropped, and figure out what you need to change going forward.

TEN OF SWORDS

Upright: end of troubles, finality, relief, peace, moving on from difficulty

A conflict finally comes to an end or a nagging problem is solved. There may or may not be a feeling of victory, but the end is welcome regardless. The need to let go of negativity associated with the old struggle and make peace with the outcome. Any needed healing or restoration can now take place. A reminder that endings are needed to make way for new beginnings.

Reversed: defeat, loss, dramatic or harsh endings, inability to move on

A harsh defeat has taken place, but the worst is over now. The need to accept the new reality in order to regroup and move on. Take a break, heal your wounds, and wait until the time is right to rebuild with a clear mind and a clean slate. As a side meaning, resisting the natural disintegration of a social group (friends or coworkers) even when it's ultimately in your best interests.

PAGE OF SWORDS

Upright: curiosity, intelligence, perception, diplomacy, truth

Taking on new studies or training. An apprenticeship or other hands-on learning situation. A person who is inquisitive, determined, logical, self-assertive, and/or honest, as well as impulsive. Learning to be diplomatic when speaking the truth. A message that's difficult to hear. The need to accept difficult truths in order to move on. Vigilance and discretion with respect to potential gossip or people with contrary or insincere motives.

Reversed: gullibility, unfinished or abandoned ventures

Losing steam too early in a project or educational program. Difficulty with studies or with ascertaining the truth about a situation. Seeking truth amid an atmosphere of purposeful deceit. Be alert for subtle misinformation intentionally thrown your way, or important information withheld, and consider new agreements very carefully.

KNIGHT OF SWORDS

Upright: discovery, intelligence, competence, haste. A sharp eye for important details. Seeking rational and logical solutions to a dilemma.

Sudden action or swiftly moving events. An energetic, focused, and decisive person. Courage and determination. May indicate that someone is acting rashly to achieve a goal without first considering all possible outcomes.

Reversed: recklessness, impulsivity, impatience, disregard for consequences

Action without thought. Undisciplined energy. Someone demonstrating a quick temper and a high degree of impulsivity. Carelessness with regard to the consequences for others of one's actions. Enjoying chaos for the sake of chaos.

QUEEN OF SWORDS

Upright: independence, perception, objectivity, intellect

Cutting away what no longer serves, whether a relationship, a plan, or habits of thinking. Coming to a sudden and profound understanding. Victory over puzzling obstacles. Taking an organized, objective, methodical approach to tasks and projects. A person who displays the qualities of strength, patience, intelligence, intellect and/or wit. Someone who is loyal, but also protective of their interests. Can indicate a widow or a mature single woman.

Reversed: isolation, control, micromanaging, ruthlessness

Independence to the point of isolation. A refusal to let others contribute to a group effort due to the need for control. Over-dependence on the intellectual mind without listening to the heart. Inability to see a wider view on an issue. Someone who is controlling, domineering, and possibly even cruel.

KING OF SWORDS

Upright: intellect, knowledge, diplomacy, analysis, perspective
The ability to fully understand a complex situation. A rational, detached, or impartial viewpoint.

A person who demonstrates independence, authority, power and/or decisiveness, but is also diplomatic. A knowledgeable, contemplative, and incisive person with a strong analytical intellect. Often relates to professionals in law or politics As a side meaning, can refer to legal or contractual matters, or official documents.

Reversed: loss of perspective, cruelty, ruthlessness

A tendency to overthink a problem until perspective is lost. An inability to see what's right in front of you. A lack of sensitivity or emotion which can lead to cruel actions. Opposition and confrontation. A win-at-all-costs mentality.

THE SUIT OF PENTACLES

Pentacles represent manifestation, and this suit is concerned with the material plane. While often relating to matters of home and money, they also speak to issues around balance, power, control, and the skillful use of talents and resources.

When many Pentacles appear in a reading, the indication is that some kind of result is either taking shape presently or already manifest. Many of the cards relate to rewards for hard work, while others may highlight fears around material insecurity.

Key words used often in association with Pentacles: manifestation, realization, fruition, proof, prosperity, security, reward.

ACE OF PENTACLES

Upright: material success, manifestation, prosperity, contentment

Potential for abundance, material well-being and security. New opportunities for financial gain and/or an upgrade in living conditions, such as buying a home. A comfortable, prosperous time and auspicious for new business or career pursuits. Never doubt your ability to manifest what you desire. Good health and general well-being are indicated.

Reversed: lost opportunity, financial loss, risk, discontent

Potential problems with money, due to external causes or to overspending. Plans may not be grounded enough in physical reality. Not an auspicious time to take financial or career risks. Potential for issues with physical health. May also indicate too much focus on materialism, at the expense of more intangible but equally important aspects of life.

TWO OF PENTACLES

Upright: balance, adaptability, time management, resourcefulness

Uncertain times concerning money or career are temporary and you are in position to use change to your advantage. Trust in your material well-being but be responsible. Balance of finances, balancing work and play. Juggling resources, particularly related to time, energy, and money. Learning a new skill. Choices involving business or career matters.

Reversed: imbalance, overwhelm, disorganization, money worries

Lack of energy or enthusiasm for meeting new challenges. Disorganized finances. Funds may be low, leading to fear and a lack-based mentality. Potential issues with a business or romantic partner over money. Avoid excess spending or imbalanced behavior. Take care of yourself and do what you can to alleviate stress responsibly.

THREE OF PENTACLES

Upright: creativity, recognition, skill, achievement

Success, particularly in business or career. Mastery in specific skills is indicated and efforts are materially rewarded. Gaining recognition from others for your talents and abilities. You may also rise in rank or status among your peers. Potential for a new home or business location, or simply an upswing in your enthusiasm and productivity.

Reversed: creative block, insufficient effort

Missed opportunities due to insufficient focused effort. Too much dreaming about long-term results at the expense of applying yourself daily to the work at hand. Remember that achievement is the result of slow and steady progress. Feeling creatively blocked and needing new inspiration. Efforts to acquire property may be delayed at this time.

FOUR OF PENTACLES

<u>Upright:</u> security, balance, protecting resources, reticence

Economic stability and firm foundations. Affirmation that you are on the right track with material resources or business investments. Abundance is assured, provided resources are allocated wisely. Remembering that abundance is a moving energy with ebb and flow. This is as much about not becoming miserly as it is about not overspending. Being reserved financially and/or socially.

<u>Reversed:</u> materialism, greed, stagnant resources, limitation

Being overly concerned with the material world. Feeling that there is never enough in terms of resources (money, time, etc.). Spending extravagantly or unwisely. Resenting the success of others. Selfish or miserly attitudes. Remember that a hoarding mentality makes true abundance stagnant. You need to be willing to release the old to make room for the new. As a side meaning, can indicate a windfall due to external circumstances, like an inheritance.

FIVE OF PENTACLES

<u>Upright:</u> insecurity, isolation, financial loss, worry, poverty, hardship

Actual financial hardship or simply a strong fear of poverty that prevents joy. Unexpected expenses may arise. Possible need to dip into savings or reconfigure your budget. Feeling "left out" of the good life that others experience. Inability to see good fortune due to focusing on lack. Poverty consciousness. Keep your focus on the evidence of abundance you already have. You will emerge from this uncomfortable place with better prospects. As a side meaning, you may need to learn to accept help from others.

Reversed: relief from financial stress, interesting opportunities

Financial hardships come to an end. New sources of income or assistance emerge, possibly from surprising places. You may be taking an unconventional approach to overcoming obstacles. Can also indicate a "spiritual poverty" due to over-focusing on the material realm, or lack of self-worth.

SIX OF PENTACLES

Upright: a gift, generosity, bonus, fair exchange

A material gain, often unexpected, either as an expression of appreciation for hard work or simply inspired generosity. This may be in the form of money, but can also be a gift, such as being taken out to dinner. Depending on the reading, you may be the giver or the receiver of this gift. Either way, there is an implied reciprocity in the energy of this exchange: neither party feels they owe anything to the other, and the giver benefits as much as the receiver.

Reversed: selfishness, debt, greed, envy, dishonest dealings

An energy of lack or perceived unfairness in material matters. Feeling slighted in an exchange. A miserly attitude toward others. Someone may be withholding assets or being otherwise dishonest in a deal, so investigate further before making any commitments. This card may also indicate troubles with debt, though the worry over it may be a bigger obstacle than the debt itself.

SEVEN OF PENTACLES

Upright: perseverance, faith, reward, profit, investment

Having faith in the long term outcome of your efforts. The need for patience with developments. Trust that the seeds of your desired results are well planted, and will bear fruit beyond your current expectations. A brief pause in effort may be needed, but don't lose momentum and don't try to rush things. A shrewd investment of time, money, or other resources.

Reversed: limited success, material insecurity, limited reward, procrastination

A temporary ebb in the unfolding of events. Worrying needlessly about the pace of progress. Lacking faith in your endeavors. Seeing minimal rewards for your efforts or investments thus far. Making unwise choices or procrastinating due to anxiety over money or other aspects of material security. Inability to visualize long-term results.

EIGHT OF PENTACLES

Upright: skilled work, studies, apprenticeship, long-term prosperity, satisfaction

An integration of creative passions or spiritual pursuits with material security. Long-term projects are maturing or manifesting on a new level. A focus on craftsmanship and pursuing mastery of a skill or talent. Satisfaction and taking pride in your work. New opportunities for advancement toward long-term career or financial goals.

Reversed: lack of long-term vision, perfectionism, dissatisfaction

Feeling trapped in a career situation that isn't satisfying or doesn't serve your long-term interests. Being disengaged at work or uninterested in current pursuits. Perfectionism and excessive self-criticism in an endeavor keeps you from learning from your mistakes. If you truly feel you are on the wrong path, now is a good time to start evaluating options.

NINE OF PENTACLES

Upright: success, self-esteem, self-confidence, rewards, good luck, prosperity, comfort

Prosperity is well-developed and humming right along. Enjoying the rewards of your work. Returns on investments (of time, effort, etc. as well as money). Good luck or an unexpected boon is on the way. Having the resources to make future gains. Enjoying the little things in life and being in the moment. Success is assured. As a side meaning, enjoying successful self-employment.

Reversed: disharmony, fear of loss, financial setbacks

Money problems jeopardizing financial security. Arguments about finances are straining relationships. Not thinking clearly about the long-term implications for how you allocate your resources. Lacking confidence in your investments. Potential health issues.

TEN OF PENTACLES

Upright: home, family, generations, wealth, inheritance, stable and secure abundance

General and consistent well-being, particularly within the family and in relation to the home. Buying, renovating, or otherwise investing in a home. Possible inheritance or other benefit from prior generations such as tuition for education. Generous friends or relatives. Wise planning for the future.

Reversed: financial failure, loss, family conflict, issues with the home, gambling

Money issues, perhaps relating to wills and inheritance, or other long-term expectations that don't come to fruition. Conflict within the family, often over money or long-term planning. Problems with the physical structure of a home or with acquiring a home. Can also indicate problems with gambling.

PAGE OF PENTACLES

Upright: financial opportunity, worthwhile effort, reliability, diligence

Good news about money, possibly via a new job. A person who demonstrates hard work, maturity, diligence, and responsibility. A student pursuing a new course of study, with a high probability of financial success if sufficiently interested to follow through. The energy of success. As a side meaning, the possible birth of children or grandchildren.

Reversed: lack of progress, short-term focus, irresponsibility, dissatisfaction

Feeling the rewards of a job or career are not worth the effort. Lacking the ability to put in the work necessary to manifest the goal. Having unrealistic goals and unfocused plans. Someone who is more interested in appearances than substance.

KNIGHT OF PENTACLES

Upright: stability, security, progress, reliability, prudent action

Good luck with money or a career development is on the horizon, likely as a result of past efforts and decisions. Dependability and attention to detail. Methodical but steady progress. A reliable and honorable person who is grounded and responsible. One who demonstrates loyalty, dedication, prudent action, and/or self-reliance.

Reversed: laziness, inaction, dishonesty, unreliability, rigidity

Inconsistent efforts. Succumbing to procrastination. Lack of willingness to put in the necessary work. Overlooking important details in the day-to-day operations of an enterprise or path of study. A person who doesn't pull their weight or tries to pass their workload onto others. As a side note, can indicate that someone is too rigid or methodical and needs to relax or change things up a little.

QUEEN OF PENTACLES

Upright: tranquility, security, generosity, abundance, satisfaction

Peace and tranquility. Relaxing into and enjoying a well-rounded abundance. Satisfaction with fruits of one's efforts or labor. A model of success due to thoughtful planning and follow-through. Someone who is accomplished, practical, and consistent. Demonstrating the qualities of generosity, thoughtfulness, dignity, and/or self-sufficiency. Someone who helps others and has a mindset that there is plenty to go around.

Reversed: selfishness, lack mentality, envy, greed, miserliness, impracticality

Lack of generosity. A person who withholds money and/or support due to insecurity or trust issues. Trying to control every aspect of one's abundance rather than trusting in the flow of it. Conversely, may also indicate a problem of over-generosity or inflated sense of financial well-being and giving away resources without first making sure there's enough to go around.

KING OF PENTACLES

Upright: economic power, sovereignty, success, security, generosity

Harnessing the energy of success. Financial sovereignty. Plans realized and manifestation completed. Wealth and abundance are secured. A highly experienced and accomplished person. A person who is generous, compassionate, responsible, and/or steadfast. Can relate to real estate and financial planning concerns. Pay attention, be practical, and seek advice from an accomplished expert in these realms.

Reversed: impracticality, lack of success, self-doubt, insecurity, greed

Success may be minimal or inconsistent due to entrenched patterns of procrastination or self-doubt. Being guarded about one's "secrets of success" and unwilling to help others thrive. The potential for greed and corruption. In an employment situation, a possible warning about a higher-up who demonstrates dishonorable or selfish behavior.

CONCLUSION

Now that you've gained a basic understanding of the Tarot, you can chart a path of your own, by exploring different spreads, building on your knowledge through further resources (you'll find a list of suggestions on the following page), and just enjoying spending time with the cards.

Remember to trust your intuition along the way. Pay attention to the ideas that pop into your mind, and to the way that you feel when interacting with the cards. Don't doubt your instincts just because instructions in a book contradict what you're picking up on.

It takes time to become a fluid reader of the Tarot, but it's a fulfilling journey. Once you get comfortable with your deck and get more practice, you'll have more and more moments when the cards are clearly speaking to you directly. When this happens, take notes on your readings and go back to them later to see which of your interpretations were most accurate.

Ultimately, you'll deepen your understanding of the cards through your own experience of life. And ideally, you'll enrich your experience of life through exploring the Tarot!

SUGGESTIONS FOR
FURTHER READING

When you're ready to take your study of the Tarot to the next level, the following resources can help you expand your knowledge. This is just a brief list, so be sure to explore further on your own!

Mary K. Greer, *21 Ways to Read a Tarot Card* (2006)

Barbara Moore, *Tarot Spreads: Layouts and Techniques to Empower Your Readings* (2012)

Robert M. Place, *The Tarot: History, Symbolism, and Divination* (2005)

Rachel Pollack, *Seventy-Eight Degrees of Wisdom: A Tarot Journey to Self-Awareness (A New Edition of the Tarot Classic)* (2019)

Christine Payne Towler, *The Underground Stream: Esoteric Tarot Revealed* (1999)

Benebell Wen, *Holistic Tarot: An Approach to Using Tarot for Personal Growth* (2015)

FREE AUDIOBOOK PROMOTION

Don't forget, you can now enjoy a **free audiobook** when you start a free 30-day trial with Audible.

If you're interested in divination, *Tarot for Beginners* covers the origins of Tarot, a comprehensive overview of the 78 cards and their meanings, and tips for beginning readers. Download for free here:

www.wiccaliving.com/free-tarot-audiobook

Or, if you'd like to learn another form of divination, *Runes for Beginners* is a great bet, with a thorough introduction to the origins and meanings of these ancient mystical symbols, including their divinatory interpretations and their uses in magic. Simply visit:

www.wiccaliving.com/free-runes-audiobook

Members receive free audiobooks every month, as well as exclusive discounts. And, if you don't want to continue with Audible, just remember to cancel your membership. You won't be charged a cent, and you'll get to keep your books!

Happy listening!

MORE BOOKS BY
LISA CHAMBERLAIN

Wicca for Beginners: A Guide to Wiccan Beliefs, Rituals, Magic, and Witchcraft

Wicca Book of Spells: A Book of Shadows for Wiccans, Witches, and Other Practitioners of Magic

Wicca Herbal Magic: A Beginner's Guide to Practicing Wiccan Herbal Magic, with Simple Herb Spells

Wicca Book of Herbal Spells: A Book of Shadows for Wiccans, Witches, and Other Practitioners of Herbal Magic

Wicca Candle Magic: A Beginner's Guide to Practicing Wiccan Candle Magic, with Simple Candle Spells

Wicca Book of Candle Spells: A Book of Shadows for Wiccans, Witches, and Other Practitioners of Candle Magic

Wicca Crystal Magic: A Beginner's Guide to Practicing Wiccan Crystal Magic, with Simple Crystal Spells

Wicca Book of Crystal Spells: A Book of Shadows for Wiccans, Witches, and Other Practitioners of Crystal Magic

Tarot for Beginners: A Guide to Psychic Tarot Reading, Real Tarot Card Meanings, and Simple Tarot Spreads

Runes for Beginners: A Guide to Reading Runes in Divination, Rune Magic, and the Meaning of the Elder Futhark Runes

Wicca Moon Magic: A Wiccan's Guide and Grimoire for Working Magic with Lunar Energies

Wicca Wheel of the Year Magic: A Beginner's Guide to the Sabbats, with History, Symbolism, Celebration Ideas, and Dedicated Sabbat Spells

Wicca Kitchen Witchery: A Beginner's Guide to Magical Cooking, with Simple Spells and Recipes

Wicca Essential Oils Magic: A Beginner's Guide to Working with Magical Oils, with Simple Recipes and Spells

Wicca Elemental Magic: A Guide to the Elements, Witchcraft, and Magical Spells

Wicca Magical Deities: A Guide to the Wiccan God and Goddess, and Choosing a Deity to Work Magic With

Wicca Living a Magical Life: A Guide to Initiation and Navigating Your Journey in the Craft

Magic and the Law of Attraction: A Witch's Guide to the Magic of Intention, Raising Your Frequency, and Building Your Reality

Wicca Altar and Tools: A Beginner's Guide to Wiccan Altars, Tools for Spellwork, and Casting the Circle

Wicca Finding Your Path: A Beginner's Guide to Wiccan Traditions, Solitary Practitioners, Eclectic Witches, Covens, and Circles

Wicca Book of Shadows: A Beginner's Guide to Keeping Your Own Book of Shadows and the History of Grimoires

Modern Witchcraft and Magic for Beginners: A Guide to Traditional and Contemporary Paths, with Magical Techniques for the Beginner Witch

FREE GIFT REMINDER

Just a reminder that Lisa is giving away an exclusive, free spell book as a thank-you gift to new readers!

Little Book of Spells contains ten spells that are ideal for newcomers to the practice of magic, but are also suitable for any level of experience.

Read it on read on your laptop, phone, tablet, Kindle or Nook device by visiting:

<u>www.wiccaliving.com/bonus</u>

DID YOU ENJOY
TAROT FOR BEGINNERS?

Thanks so much for reading this book! I know there are many great books out there about the Tarot, so I really appreciate you choosing this one.

If you enjoyed the book, I have a small favor to ask—would you take a couple of minutes to leave a review for this book on Amazon?

Your feedback will help me to make improvements to this book, and to create even better ones in the future. It will also help me develop new ideas for books on other topics that might be of interest to you. Thanks in advance for your help!

CPSIA information can be obtained
at www.ICGtesting.com
Printed in the USA
BVHW081324300720
585015BV00005B/14

9 781912 715046